THE BLACK REVOLTS:
RACIAL STRATIFICATION IN THE U.S.A.

The Politics of Estate, Caste, and Class
in the American Society

by
Joseph W. Scott

SCHENKMAN PUBLISHING COMPANY, INC.
Cambridge, Massachusetts

DEDICATED
TO PAST, PRESENT AND FUTURE
AMERICAN FREEDOM FIGHTERS
AND ESPECIALLY VICTOR, VALLI,
AND VELISSA

Copyright © 1976

Schenkman Publishing Company, Inc.
3 Mt. Auburn Place
Cambridge, Massachusetts 02138

LIBRARY OF CONGRESS
CATALOG CARD NO.: 76-9683

ISBN 87073-208-0 cloth
        87073-209-9 paper

Printed in the United States of America

ACKNOWLEDGEMENTS

I am endebted to the following scholars and friends: Joyce Ladner, Mary Berry, John H. Clarke, James Turner, Robert Perry, Louis Killian, Sidney Willhelm, Larry Reynolds, and James Geshwender who encouraged and criticized my work as it progressed over the years.

ACKNOWLEDGMENTS

Contents

Preface

The primary purpose of this book is to inform antiracists, both inside and outside academe, about the nature and function of institution-alized racism in the United States. I hope to elucidate the critical forces which the white power elite has used in systematic ways throughout the history of the United States to subjugate the black population of the American society.

It would be too simplistic to attribute the misery of black Americans to a few individual racists who derive some type of ego gratification or status elevation from oppressing blacks. It would also be too simplis-tic to say that black depredation is caused by a few prejudiced lowly whites who need to have some group to which to feel superior. Psycho-logical forces are important, to be sure, but they do not account for the systematic establishment of a social system of racial etiquette and racial practices, because such psychological forces do not account for the actions of unprejudiced persons who have directed the plantations and corporations which have systematically extracted great profits from the exploitation of black laborers and consumers.

Economic and social gains themselves most obviously have been primary motivations of white persons for systematically exploiting blacks. Ironically it has become profitable in recent days to be an equal-opportunity employer, so the leaders of government and indus-try have been willing to modify their racial practices to place blacks in some favorable situations. The profit motive, interpreted quite broadly, is still the most certain reason behind these moves. Even educated, cultivated, and racially unprejudiced persons have been willing, along with racists, to exploit blacks when it has been profitable. Exploitation is so integral to the system of politics, economics, education, and social etiquette that discriminators themselves have often said that it is not a personal matter—it is just a part of doing a job. Thus it is time we looked for institutionalized structures of behavior which require racial discrimination as a matter of role definition within the public and private bureaucracies, in which both prejudiced and unprejudiced individuals are rewarded for racially discriminating. It is time we recognized that many individuals in such bureaucracies carry out economic and social exploitation of blacks as routine parts of their daily work.

The survey of the historical data herein indicates that the key mechanisms for the development and maintenance of systematic economic and social exploitation have been political and economic in character. The data indicate that legal-political differentiation of blacks and whites preceded their socio-economic differentiation. Furthermore, legal-political discrimination led to political-economic discrimination and further to social discimination. The racial "estates" of whites over blacks emerged as a result of a series of legislative acts and court decisions. Economic advantages for whites became unearned, inevitable outcomes of the legal-political restrictions and deprivations imposed on blacks. Without these legal-political straightjackets, the type of economic exploitation exemplified, for example, by chattel slavery, in which blacks were forced to be economically inferior to whites, could not have come about. The racist laws gave whites the *right* to exploit blacks for profit. Since all races have innately talented members who will excel, given open opportunities, the collective subordination of one racial group to another in a society such as ours requires legal-political force. The historical data on blacks in the United States indicate that this is a valid sociological conclusion.

What the white builders of American society did three hundred years ago would be comparable to a reorganization of the contemporary National Football League along racial lines. If all blacks were grouped together in teams and given the opportunity to learn the playing positions and perform all the managerial roles, many whites would find themselves on the losing side. In order to win consistently, white players would have to contrive a system which would restrict blacks from learning the playing positions and practicing the managerial professions. They would also have to restrict blacks altogether from playing, or they would have to concoct a discriminatory system so that black teams would always be put at a disadvantage in terms of field position, penalties, and points for touchdowns, field goals, and safeties. In short, in order for whites to insure victory all the time, they would have to structure the game and the opportunities for playing and managing so that each black team in all probability would be forced to lose each game to the white team they played. Given the range of talent within the black race, only a legal-political contrivance would produce white over black victories in perpetuity.

In the society at large, the white founders of this nation contrived a social system comparable to the hypothetical one I just described. The losing performances by blacks in political, economic, educational, and social spheres have been a result of the legal-political restrictions set up by whites to guarantee white success and black failure in all areas of life in which blacks and whites would be potential competitors. Legal and customary curbs on equal education, training, competition, trading, and capitalization are still being used to perpetuate the white-over-black system. The historical data make it clear that racial stratification in the United States has been an outcome of institutionalized racial discrimination designed to insure white success and black failure, and contemporary studies indicate that political mechanisms still provide whites with the opportunities for economic and social discrimination, exploitation and subordination of blacks.

The "race problem" in the United States has not been nor is it today *at its base* an economic problem. At base, the race problem has been a legal-political problem in which blacks and whites have been assigned to separate legal "estates," i.e. legal categories wherein racists have passed laws which guarantee to whites every conceivable economic advantage over blacks.

After racist politicians forcibly relegated blacks to the disadvantaged, disenfranchised estate wherein their innate talents and potentialities were suppressed by "law and order," the oppressed had no other choices but to die accepting oppression or to live trying to overthrow the system. "Law and order" provisions forced blacks into a servile status, and "law and order" have kept blacks down. To respect this "law and order" has been tantamount to tacit approval of an oppressive system. Many blacks have chosen to reject both the system and its racist rules of "law and order." They have revolted.

The comment "No matter how much you strive and no matter how much money you amass in the United States—if you're black, you're still a nigger," is understandable in this context of legal estates. The legal condition predetermines economic success and failure and takes precedence where the two come in conflict. This is why the black bourgeoisie found itself inescapably tied to the black proletarians. Consequently, it has been misleading to tell blacks that an improvement of their economic status would mean an automatic improvement in their legal and political status. The black bourgeoisie has learned painfully that this is not the case. Even with money, the black bourgeoisie suffered both the legal-political and the social restrictions. The eradication of the legal-political and social restrictions, they learned, had to be carried out by legal-political assaults, rather than individual economic improvement.

When one investigates the black revolts of the 1960's and relates them to the black revolts of previous centuries, the pattern that emerges is one of blacks attacking in a rational and purposeful direction. Since 1660, the chief concern of blacks has been institutionalized white racism, and black activists have been striving to change this situation through acts of revolution or reformation. The basic rational and moral purpose behind the black revolts has been to liberate the oppressed: themselves. It would be dishonest to say that blacks have not been about the business of overturning the white-over-black estates, for they have, and they have used litigation, legislation, emigration, demonstration, rebellion, destruction, assimilation, separation, education, commercialization, and coalition in their attempts to overturn the system of black-white estates and they have succeeded in part. They have sought a new institutional order, a new relationship to whites. They have, in three hundred years, changed that basic relationship somewhat. What blacks have been about for all these years is what they are about today: The liberation struggle is the message.

The present socio-economically disadvantaged position of blacks in the United States makes future revolts inevitable. The aspirations of blacks are the same as they were three hundred years ago. The struggle for success in a society which tries to make them fail is the same struggle. The strategies of revolt are the same, but updated for the historical time and situation.

In the following chapters I describe the basic nature and function of racial estates in the United States, the ways in which black revolts have been changing that system for the past three hundred years, and how they can continue to change that system in the decades to come.

Introduction: The Racial Estates

The Kerner Report of 1967 claimed that presently "our nation is moving toward two societies, one white and one black—separate and unequal."[1] But in a more accurate sense, we have long been two separate "societies" or, more properly, two separate racial "estates"* since about 1660—for more than three hundred years. Ever since whites legalized slavery for blacks only, we have been a system of legal "estates"—status groups, political categories, legal orders.[2] These past three hundred years have therefore been filled with racial conspiracies and racial strife. All this time, whites and blacks have been continually confronting each other as separate and opposed legal estates. Hence race relations in the United States have been pointedly of one character—conflict, either overt or covert.

"With the exception of a brief period after the Civil War, the pattern of American Negro-white relationships, especially in the American South, closely approximated the classic accommodative pattern of superordination-subordination, with the whites a continually dominant group. The most savage oppression, whether expressed in rural lynchings and pogroms or in urban race riots, has taken place when the Negro refused to accept a subordinate status. The most intense

*In sociological terminology "estate" denotes a set of legalized social statuses or ranks. In this study the term refers to a set of legal-political and socioeconomic groupings of persons to whom are ascribed superior and inferior statuses or ranks by law. Its usually imposed on the powerless bv those with a monopoly of power.

conflict has resulted when the subordinate minority attempted to disrupt the accommodative pattern or when the superordinate group defined the situation as one in which such an attempt was being made. Conflict in Negro-white relationships in the United States has been conflict generated by the breakdown of an essentially unstable accommodative pattern, essentially unstable because the subordinated group has refused to accept its status and has had sufficient power to challenge" it.[3]

For one short generation, it was possible for racially distinguishable Africans and Europeans—blacks and whites—to coexist peaceably. But, as often happens in human relationships, absolute power corrupts. Blacks and whites became separate and unequal racial estates as white racist leaders—who were more numerous, wealthier, and in absolute control of the political means of force and violence—decided to impose a despotic system on blacks and to assign to themselves only all the worthwhile social privileges, economic advantages, and political rights while denying the same to blacks. Having a monopoly of force and violence, the whites were able to back up their legal decrees with force and also went a step further: they audaciously assigned themselves to a higher human order of worth and dignity. The move from nonracial estates to racial estates set into motion institutionalized racism in the U.S.

"While the importation of Negro labor into this country began in 1619, the Negro's status as a member of a legal group was only gradually defined. It is only with a clarification of the Negro's status as being a legal one, rather than one of social class, that it becomes legitimate to speak of Negro-white relationships.[4]"

As their wealth and control grew, whites eventually ascribed to themselves the highest human worth and ascribed to blacks the lowest human worth: that of brute property. Whites eventually convinced themselves—not blacks—of this duality.

Slavery was such a "complete loss of liberty that it seemed to Englishmen somehow akin to loss of humanity. No theme was more persistent than the claim that to treat a man as a slave was to treat him as a beast."[5]

Starting with a system of indentured servitude, gradually the white founders of this nation ascribed to all whites privileges of the master estate, whether they were masters or not, and at the same time, they forced on blacks the degradation of perpetual servitude.[6]

Those blacks who had already been freed from indentures were reduced to near-slaves: subordinated, disenfranchised, and pushed aside (for the most part) to the wastelands of the United States.

Through the systematic use of law, police power, and unrestrained mob violence, racist leaders were able to subjugate blacks, turning once peacefully coexisting white and black individuals into collectivities of conflicting, warring estates. As this came to pass, whites and blacks became unified legalized racial orders assigned different legal privileges and levels of social esteem, and notions of biological superiority and inferiority were conjured up to justify this racial discrimination.

When these racial statuses were made legally hereditary, white advantages and black disadvantages, unearned and undeserved, became involuntary and unchangeable. Having legally bound blacks to interminable servitude, whites set about the task of consolidating their power and perpetuating their economic and political advantages as well as their social privileges. Not being psychologically convinced of their "innate superiority", they strove to make themselves materially and socially superior in all those conspicuous areas of life where black and white individuals could allegedly symbolize their innate worth. As servitude became hereditary by social law and economic success a consequence of the law, what was a fiction of racial superiority eventually became "real". Accordingly, the weaker and less intelligent members of the white estate had to be "given" the minimum financial rewards and privileges even when they were incapable of earning them. Thus through law and social contrivances biological superiority too was imposed, but it must be remembered that it was engineered through the polity, not through biology. To make it "real," whites methodically established social differences between the races in all areas of life—economic, familial, religious, educational, political, and legal.

After gradually separating white and black citizens into separate legal orders, white leaders further imposed prohibitions against intermingling and marriage, supported by doctrines of racial separatism. Whites and blacks were to be kept both socially separate and racially distinct.

Whites have used three dominant legal-political systems in the past three hundred years of black subjugation: white despotism, jim crowism, and token integrationism. These three doctrines have provided the legal-political basis for the establishment and maintenance of three exploitive economic systems: chattel slavery, debt peonage, and wage peonage.

In liberating themselves, blacks have assaulted the system with three dominant political-economic counterdoctrines. They attacked chattel slavery and white despotism through black abolitionism. They attacked debt peonage and jim crowism through black assimilationism, involving two phases of abolition-assimilation activity. And, finally, they attacked wage peonage and token integrationism through black separatism. Such has been the interactional nature of black-white relations in the United States.

The Legal-Political Basis of Black Subjugation and Exploitation
    Legal-political measures were the most important means of subjugating black people. Complete economic servility was made possible only through legal-political promotion, protection and perpetuation. Laws and law-enforcement personnel, more than any other measures (even economic), brought about the "thinghood" of blacks. The following laws are cases in point:

> Slaves shall be deemed, sold, taken, reputed and adjudged in law to be chattels personal, in the hands of their owners and possessors, and their executors, administrators and assigns, to all intents, constructions, and purposes whatsoever. (South Carolina)[7]
> A slave is one who is in the power of a master to whom he belongs. The master may sell him, dispose of his person, his industry and his labor. He can do nothing, possess nothing, not acquire anything, but what must belong to his master. (Louisiana)[8]

Through various legal-political measures, whites assigned and enforced a condition of "thinghood" on blacks, wiping out all their previously held legal-bases of personhood, material possessions, social privileges, and human rights. The legal-political agents who founded this nation forcibly stopped blacks from exercising any free will, free spirit, or freedom of movement. The polity reduced black human beings to brutes who were not even allowed to own themselves or their children. Like animals, they had no right of selfhood, personhood, brotherhood or fatherhood. Blacks were legislated property and they were no longer to be political *beings* in human society. Consider the following interpretation of the slave condition:

The slave cannot be considered by the Government as entitled to its protection while he is not regarded by it as having any right to be protected. And the Government that recognizes and protects slave chattelhood has already, in that very act, denied to the slave the possession of any rights by denying to him the right of self-ownership *which is the foundation and parent stock of all other rights, and without which they cannot exist.*

Having no right to himself, to his bones, muscles, and intellect, (being all of them the property of his "owner") he has no right to his own industry, to its wages or its products; no right to property or capability of possessing it, as already shown. Of course he has no right of property *to be protected by the Government, and none of the rights that grow out of them.*

Having no recognized right of making any contract, he has no contracts with others to be enforced by the Government, and no one has any legal pecuniary claims upon him to be enforced. He can neither sue nor be sued. This is no arbitrary rule. It is the inevitable result of his chattelhood.[9]

Economic servility was a necessary consequence of legal-political servility. It could not have been otherwise. Economic factors like supply, demand, price costs, capital, and practices of buying, selling, hiring, and borrowing could not have subjugated every black so completely, so totally, and so lastingly. Market factors themselves, unguided by racism, would have produced a more equal distribution of money, power, position, and personal esteem between the races. But legal-political contrivances and armed force created the basis for the economic subjugation of blacks, and these same legal-political contrivances and forces have kept blacks in that position. The white-over-black system was first and foremost a political entity.

Freeborn blacks were as much objects of oppression as enslaved blacks. In Virginia, freeborn blacks were restricted by law in numerous ways[10]:

- 1670 a law was enacted prohibiting free blacks from purchasing white servants.
- 1723 free blacks were forbidden to keep or carry guns, gunpowder, shot, or clubs, even to defend themselves.
- 1785 a statute discontinued the right of free blacks to be witnesses even in civil suits in which a white man was plaintiff against a black defendant.
- 1793 free blacks were forbidden to enter the state of Virginia for the purpose of taking up permanent residence. They could not go from county to county seeking employment without a passport.
- 1813 a special poll tax was levied on free blacks.
- 1831 free blacks were denied the right of trial by jury except for offences punishable by death.

- 1832 free blacks were forbidden to purchase slaves for profit-making purposes; though they could purchase relatives.
- 1843 free blacks were forbidden to own dogs.
- 1848 no free black could leave the state for purposes of education and return.

In South Carolina, if a freed black entertained a runaway slave, be it his own child or wife, he could be reenslaved. In Virginia if the freed slaves remained for twelve months, in the state after emancipation, they could be reenslaved. In Maryland a freed black who married a white woman could be reenslaved. In Georgia every freed black who came into the state and was unable to pay a fine of one hundred dollars became a slave for life. In Virginia, as in Georgia, Alabama, and South Carolina, gatherings of Negroes for the purpose of instruction in reading and writing were unlawful assemblies. In Louisiana freed blacks could not insult or strike white people, nor presume themselves to be equal to whites. In Kentucky if a freed black lifted his or her hand in opposition to any person other than a Negro, mulatto, or Indian, he or she was punished with thirty lashes on the bare back. Because they were not citizens by federal law, freed blacks were often neither permitted land grants nor the purchase of government land.

In sum, the legal-political order predetermined the economic life chances of all blacks, not just those who were enslaved. Unrestricted competition between blacks and whites in the British-American colonies and later in the independent colonies never became a reality for any category of blacks since 1660. Black economic activity has hence forward been curtailed by the polity. Without direct political intervention in the marketplace, such economic subjugation of all blacks—freed and enslaved—could not have occurred.

In these early days of legal-political subjugation, blacks reacted with the few means they had available to them—mostly individual indignation, insubordination, and rage. Those unable or unwilling to risk life or limb, acquiesced in the hope that they, like indentured servants, would be able eventually to work their way out of slavery. A few white masters did offer conditional opportunities for manumission as ways of pacifying the slaves and motivating them to be compliant and loyal for most of their productive lives, knowing full well that after giving the best years of their lives, the slaves would be unable to support themselves if and when they were released, and hence would probably not desire their "freedom" when it came.

Many blacks, however, came to realize that neither the dominant group's powers, privileges, and honors, nor their own lack of them, followed automatically from any innate factors, or even from hard work or the lack of it. They embarked, therefore, on another course of anti-estate strategies, realizing that being of African descent and living in a despotic society of white racists were, in fact, the basic causes of black "inferiority." They also realized that they could not escape the plight of continued racial subjugation by simply working hard and trying to assimilate the white man's style of religion, clothing, grooming, manner, morals, or speech. Legal-political racism was a consequence of having sufficient legal-political power to impose it; without such power, white reaction to Africanness alone could not have continued to produce perpetual black servitude, in the face of black intellectual abilities, efforts, or motivation to advance themselves. By their own rules, whites fixed the process so that they would progress while blacks would stagnate.

Blacks came to realize that they had to acquire sufficient power to end or limit the dominant groups' arbitrary enjoyment of unearned social privileges and economic advantages; they had to end or limit their arbitrary use of biological origins to justify prohibitions on blacks developing their own innate abilities and potentialities. Fed up with forced social degradation and political and economic deprivation, more and more black freedom fighters rejected the one-sided goal of amalgamation and acculturation into the dominant society, and instead began to galvanize black racial pride and unity. Consequently in recent years as in days of slavery, blacks have increasingly and voluntarily come together to cultivate their own "black" manners, morals, identities, and institutions, based on African rather than European models. It is for some time, then, that blacks have been reviving aspects of the various African cultures once practiced in the Old and New Worlds. Black freedom fighters have started several social movements designed to unite scattered black individuals into quasi-communals and into a quasi-kinship group composed of "brothers" and "sisters." More and more over the years, light and dark members of the black estate have been subordinating their color differences and their private economic interests to the group interests and social solidarity of all "Africans." The racial interests of all "Africans in America" have begun to overshadow the interests of the separate color categories, and, with this growing collective consciousness, blacks have taken the first necessary steps for a revolutionary mass-action movement: the development of a leadership; the recruitment, coordination and control of a cadre of freedom fighters; and the dissemination of effective tactical strategies to abolish the system of racial estates.

In every historical epoch of this society, there have been socially structured opportunities for dissident blacks to attack the institutionalized estate system within that society. These assault opportunities have not always been apparent, and even when they were, dissident members have not usually been in control of sufficient means to carry out a revolution or a near-revolution. Control of the means to assault the racist institutions of the society has been limited by the social, economic, political and technological structure of the society, and the type of participation of dissidents within it. The United States, like all societies, has institutions where socially structured opportunities and the effective technology for assaulting the vulnerabilities of those institutions have existed. Blacks, however, have not known the types and locations of these opportunities and technologies and have had to experiment to find targets and means to attack the vulnerable parts of the system. They have had to probe; that is, to engage in trial and error activities to locate the vulnerabilities and to acquire the most effective knowledge and technology with which to force change in the institutionalized racial structure. Many individual acts of rebellion began as "probes" of the system which later became conscious tactics for some black mass-action movements with the effect of testing the will, power, and reactive capacity of whites. The Black Panthers constitute the best recent example of probers of the system. Valuable lessons have been learned from their example, (see Chapter 5) and blacks have adjusted their strategies accordingly.

During slavery to be sure, blacks had fewer institutionalized opportunities for assaulting the system than they have now. During slavery they were not permitted so many opportunities to assemble freely, move about, speak in public, publish papers, or bear arms. Today, by contrast, blacks have many institutionalized opportunities to attack white racism overtly, but most still do not recognize these opportunities to assault the system. The method of assault used by slaves was through various individual acts of arson, assassination, sabotage, and flight. Because only small numbers of slaves were allowed to assemble, they less frequently assaulted the racist system as large, organized collectivities. Many individual acts of rebellion nevertheless triggered mass-action tactics such as boycotts, guerilla warfare, massacres, riots, and civil disruption. Through these collective assaults, slaves were able to force the white leaders either to reform or remove some of the institutionalized mechanisms of racial oppression of that time.

For those who doubt that there have been many vulnerabilities in the American system of racial estates, and for those who doubt that these vulnerabilities have become opportunities for blacks to assault the system, we offer the cases of David Walker, Denmark Vesey, Frederick Douglass, Martin Luther King, Jr., and Huey Newton for their consideration. Their acts of defiance and rebellion have demonstrated that viable strategies for change do exist. They helped to determine which strategies would work and how they would work, and these in turn became diffused by word of mouth and from hand to hand. Other dissident organizers of the black masses then adopted the new tactical concepts they had heard of or had seen in operation. In time, groups like the American Mau Mau, the NAACP, the Black Panthers and the SCLC emerged and concertedly moved against the institutionalized racial order.

Predictably, white countermovements have emerged to stop these black groups so that every black assault movement has eventually been slowed down or neutralized by one or more white countermovements of repression. Even with their monopoly of power and all their weapons of violence, the dominant group has never completely suppressed change or pushed all blacks back to their starting points. Neither have whites been able to roll back time once change and gain were secured. In short, blacks have always been able to make some gains during each of the assault phases, and some of the gains have been retained despite periods of white repressive reaction. These small gains then became energizing factors, motivating blacks to start new rounds of probes and assaults. Racial struggle in the U.S. has been characterized by whites shoring one set of beleaguered vulnerabilities, while blacks have been discovering and attacking still different ones. The lulls in black assaults from one period to another have been largely a result of the amount of time it has taken to probe, discover, organize, equip, and assault.

This historical cycle of repressions, probes, assaults, changes, and further repressions has persisted for three centuries; only the assault opportunities and tactics employed have changed. Belonging to different racial estates, both whites and blacks have acted in predictable ways: whites have spent their time and energy systematically repressing blacks, and blacks have spent their time and energy trying to overthrow the system. I term this historical conflict of contending racial estates "the politics of racial stratification."

Politics of Racial Estates
The keepers of the public trust—the white men who first held the

personal power, the public power, and the power of property—seized
the opportunities of their time to utilize the means of coercion, and
manipulation, both violent and nonviolent, to subjugate the most
defenseless social group—namely, black people. They conspired,
measure by measure, act by act, to control and to use black people for
their own political, economic and social gains.

Thus the keepers of the public trust planted the seeds of the black
revolts by establishing the conditions, the motives, and the goals of
what we now call "the human rights revolution." What was to follow
for the next three hundred years was predictable. Blacks were forced to
concentrate on overthrowing the white-over-black system which we
recognize today as one of institutional estates. While whites were
forced to defend racial injustice, blacks were forced to concentrate on
developing strategies for changing this system from within and without.

Finding themselves in a new land with opportunities for profit,
whites needed absolute control over the natural resources, and human
resources. Exploitation of these resources was the primary means of
capital accumulation. The white Anglo-protestant nationalist discovered that the blacks in their midst were defenseless, and they seized
them for that opportunity. In doing so, they organized the political,
economic, and social institutions along the lines of racial estates, thereby setting whites against blacks and blacks against whites. They created
a sociopolitical order with whites perpetually occupying the master
estate and blacks the servant estate. Blacks and whites respectively were
forced into a situation where they had to develop common racial sentiments and common racial strategies appropriate for dealing with this
peculiar form of society. White nationalism preceded white capitalism.

The "politics of racial stratification" specifically refers to (1) the
social, economic, and political strategies by which the whites have
sought to implement, consolidate, and maintain their superior social,
political and economic rank and the privileges and advantages which
accrue as a result; and (2) the strategies by which the blacks have
sought to wrest from the dominant group the various means of control over the instruments of power which permit whites to maintain
their unearned privileges and advantages.

The United States was founded in conflict and has been maintained
by conflict. It is changing through conflict. White-black relations
have been antagonistic from the first moment of black subjugation;
they have continued in antagonistic ways to the present.

THE BLACK REVOLTS

1 Instituting The White Over The Black Estate

The British-American leaders who first organized this nation initially instituted a politico-economic nonracial system of estates based on masters and indentured servants. They began the "American experiment" by legislating social, political, and economic distinctions between freemen and bondmen without regard to race. At that time, race was not a basis for determining either freedom or servitude. Servitude liberty and restrictions on property rights and personal privileges. tured servitude was neither servitude for life nor was it inheritable from one's parents, especially one's mother.

The white-over-black estates began when the British-American founders decided to use race as a basic organizing principle for the existing economic, political and social institutions. During the early seventeenth century the white leaders of this nation decided to change that biological descent and not biological capability would be the chief criterion for determining the level of an individual's participation in the civil, political, economic and ecclesiastical life of society. Jordan put the matter succinctly:

13

Evidently Negroes, even free Negroes, were regarded as distinct from the English. They were, in New England where economic necessities were not sufficiently pressing to determine the decision, treated differently from other men.[1]

It seems logical to suppose that this perception of the Negro as being distinct from the Englishman must have operated to debase his status rather than to raise it, for in the absence of countervailing social factors, the need for labor in the colonies usually told in the direction of non-freedom.[2]

Some historians have maintained that the white master class abhorred white slavery, even as they approved of white servitude for a limited duration. But, the fact that many white masters tried to manipulate the terms of the contracts with their white indentured servants in order to make them serve in perpetuity gives the lie to this contention. If they could have made white slavery work sociologically, without jeopardizing themselves and the solidarity of the society, the masters would have done so. But white slavery was not as workable as black slavery for several political and sociological reasons. First, between white masters and white servants there was a common identity and sympathy based on a common culture, common religion, common ancestry, and common biological appearance. Secondly, white slaves could more easily "pass" as freemen once they had taken flight from their masters, making social control more difficult. Thirdly, and perhaps most important, perpetual servitude would have permanently divided friendships and families which had been established during the years of indentured servitude. During the early generations of servitude, there had been social and sexual intercourse between the members of the two legal estates, freemen and bondmen. Therefore, confining the latter category to perpetual servitude would have divided families which had already formed and would have undermined the basic fabric of the society.

The masters were having a difficult enough time as it was, trying to attract white laborers from Europe. White enslavement of newcomers would have made ongoing recruitment impossible, as word of such practices reached Europe. Elkins maintains that the manipulations of contracts by masters made even white laborers in Europe reluctant to come to the colonies. Not to have white slavery was a sociological imperative.

To encourage the immigration of such servants and to counteract homeward drifting rumors of indefinite servitude under desperate conditions, it was becoming more and more the practice to fix definite and limited terms of indenture—five or six years—as a guarantee that a clear future awaited the white man who could cast his lot with the colonies.[3]

The first twenty blacks who were sold to the colony of Virginia were servants.[4] At that time none of the colonies had instituted slavery in an explicit and legal manner. Various masters, however, from time to time had tried to scheme and manipulate the terms of their contracts with white indentured servants so as to ensure their services for life, but this practice was frowned upon by large numbers of fellow Christians. The first twenty blacks were not to be bound for the "rest of their natural lives." Most were, in fact, permitted to work out specific and limited terms of servitude, according to which they could obtain their freedom in a specified manner. They were permitted thereafter to acquire white and black indentured servants to work for them. They also were permitted by custom and by law to mingle with other races of the same class.

Historians have concluded from the available evidence that this group of twenty Blacks exchanged for goods in Virginia in 1619 were not enslaved, but rather led servants' lives on servants' terms. Historians have also agreed that Virginia law contained no legal recognition of slavery, neither condoning slavery, regulating slavery, nor requiring slavery of any particular race. In fact, it was to be almost forty more years before slavery as such was enacted into Virginia law. The best available evidence uncovered by historians permits us to summarize the development of African slavery in the United States as follows: The first blacks to enter the colonies entered in the same manner as did many whites before them. They were sold, and it had not been uncommon for ship masters to sell white servants to planters in the colonies. Secondly, slavery was first a folkway and then became a stateway; that is it was customary before it was enacted into law. Some of the first blacks to become slaves had been servants who were forcibly or deceitfully kept in bondage. Before legislated slavery, other blacks became slaves as a result of being sentenced to perpetual bondage by the courts. Thus the first legislative acts recognizing slavery in Virginia did not institute slavery—they only regulated what was to be the status of children born to those already enslaved. Customary and judicial slavery preceded statutory slavery. Thirdly, in the midst of the practice of customary slavery, many black indentured servants obtained their freedom after the normal period of servitude. The historical records bear out this conclusion, and indicate that many freed blacks became land owners, property owners and masters over other servants. Fourthly, as the years passed, it became more and more difficult for black servants to escape perpetual servitude, because they had been sold without indentures or contracts to planters. It was difficult enough for those who had contracts to escape being reduced to perpetual servitude, but those without contracts had less and less chance of gaining freedom at all. In sum the historical records indicate that black servants were reduced to slaves by several means prior to legislation being enacted to this effect; for example, threats and coercion, deceit and misrepresentation in contracts, and racially discriminatory judicial decisions were all used to enslave blacks.

American society thus began with indentured servitude and hence two nonracial estates: masters and servants. It was a system legally defining estates of free and unfree men. Each category had its rights and privileges, and each had its obligations to the other. Race was not a basis for assigning rights, privileges, and obligations, deprivations, and degradations; nor was race a principle for the automatic exclusion of some peoples from full participation in the economic, educational, religious, political, and social institutions of the society. The terms "black American" and "white American" did not evoke the negative, hateful images they do now. Separate and distinct legal-political racial interests were not yet established and therefore violent opposition between the races had not emerged.

Blacks and whites, in essential matters, could belong to the same legal, economic, and civil statuses, and those Africans who converted to Christianity even shared the same religious status as the majority of whites. Thus in the first few years of the colonies, blacks from England, Spain, Portugal, and the West Indies came voluntarily to be bondmen and indentured servants. Many of them later became Christians and were accorded the same privileges as other Christians, for English morality and law forbade undeserved enslavement of fellow Christians. Blacks came from other countries, served their indentures, achieved their freedom, and later acquired servants of their own. Those blacks who became members of the master class acquired the same legal powers over servants as white masters of the same status. At least one black man's name is recorded in the annals of history as having imported a white man as an indentured servant, the black man serving as the white man's legal master for the duration of their contract. On the specific subject of "substantial equality," Bennett has written:

Within the confines of this system, which can only be called *equality of repression*, Negroes fared about as well as whites. They held real property and transferred it, sued in court and were sued. Some Negroes voted and a few held the minor offices of beadle and surety. In a limited sense, then, the Jamestown experience was an *open* experience. Negroes were free to express themselves according to their personalities and their different lights. They could live with white people if they wanted to, or they could live without them: and some Negroes, interestingly enough, wanted to live without them.[5]

The first blacks intermingled with whites on terms of substantial equality even though, to be sure, there was some prejudice operating at the level of individual personal preferences for color and beauty on the parts of both whites and blacks. As a case in point, the first marriage of a black man was to a black woman who bore him a child around 1625. Personal prejudices existed, but legislated racism as such, did not. It is reasonable to conclude that early United States society was substantially open; that is, the economic classes were open, and whites and blacks worked side by side in the same fields, sometimes lived in the same houses, were usually punished and esteemed in similar ways. They fraternized during their off-duty time, and some blacks even mated and married whites. Intermingling of the white and black races during these colonial days was so extensive that some travelers felt moved to comment about the high number of mulatto children running about the colonies.

Bennett has commented on colonial "integration" as follows:

Working together in the same fields, sharing the same huts, the same situation, and the same hope, the first Negro and white Americans, aristocrats excepted, developed strong bonds of sympathy and mutuality. There was no barrier, psychological or otherwise, between them; and circles of community and solidarity began to widen. Skin color had a meaning then but not the meaning it has now. The basic division was between servants and free people; and there were White and Negroes on both sides of the line. One has to make an effort to grasp the contours of this world. It seems somehow un-American, as undoubtedly it was, since it has existed in America for only one brief spell and then by default. A Negro in this world could almost feel at home. There was not the fatal split between an American, whatever that is, and being Negro, whatever that is.[6]

Approximately one generation (thirty years) passed before African slavery was first recognized by legislation. Within this original generation, several of the blacks who first arrived were able to rise from the servant to the master class. Several black servants were known to have petitioned for their freedom after a time and won it. The historian John H. Russell has reported that some of those blacks who won their freedom later became independent landowners.[7] Other historians, Oscar and Mary Handlin, James C. Ballagh, and Ulrich Phillips agree with Russell that legal slavery was not imposed on these first black settlers in America and that they were not held in perpetual servitude either through the matrilineal or partilineal line of heredity.

From Servitude to Slavery
Ballagh has traced the development of slavery as follows:

The primary steps in the institutional development which culminated in slavery are then to be found in the legislation, customary and statutory, that defined that condition of persons legally known as servitude. Servitude not only preceded slavery in the logical development of the principle of subjection, standing midway between freedom and absolute subjection, but it was the historical base upon which slavery, by the extension and addition of incidents, was constructed. Developed itself from a species of free contract-labor, by the peculiar conditions surrounding the importation of settlers and laborers into the English-American colonies, servitude was first applied to whites and then Negroes and Indians. Negro and Indian servitude thus preceded Negro and Indian slavery, and together with white servitude in instances continued even after the institution of slavery was fully developed.[8]

Virginia was not the only colony in which servitude bore this direct relation to slavery as its preparatory stage or form. Negro and Indian servitude passed historically into slavery in most of the English-American colonies, if not in all. This is certainly true of Rhode Island, Pennsylvania, Georgia, North Carolina and South Carolina. In all of these colonies statutory recognition of slavery, though tending to be anticipated by customary or judicial sanction, was postponed for some time after the introduction of the subjects of slavery, who were consequently referred to a different status.[9]

. . . Virginia, then, so far from being the first American colony to sanction domestic slavery, as has been generally believed, was in reality but the third, being preceded by both Massachusetts and Connecticut. Prior to these dates the legal status of all subject Negroes was that of servants, and their rights, duties, and disabilities were regulated by legislation the same as, or similar to, that applied to white servants.[10]

Indentured servitude was the essential forced-labor mechanism of the colonial economic system. It worked in conjunction with both the apprenticeship system and the contract-wage system, and was, without any exaggeration, the basic mode for the development of the craft and agricultural industries. To acquire laborers, the employers or their agents raided English prisons, orphanages, houses of prostitution, and slums to find able-bodied white men, women, and children. More than two-thirds of the laborers within the colonies came in under this forced-labor system at various periods during the seventeenth and eighteenth centuries.

Black slavery, however, developed more gradually and was maintained along with the maintenance of white indentured servitude. According to Jordan, 1640 marked the first instance of racial slavery, and it was by court decision:

> The General Court pronounced sentence on three servants who had been retaken after absconding to Maryland. Two of them, a Dutchman and a Scott, were ordered to serve their masters for one additional year and then the colony for three more, but the "third being a Negro named John Punch shall serve his said master or his assigns for the time of his natural life here or elsewhere." No white servant in any English colony, so far as is known, ever received a like sentence.[11]

This judicial slavery thus began the first institutionalized racial slavery. Subsequent enslavement of individual blacks apparently occurred through similar legal processes of the courts. Thus individual cases of slavery began first by custom and then by court decision. Statutory slavery soon followed the court permission of slavery. Without power and without the judicial or legal-political protection of whites, blacks were collectively, easily forced into perpetual servitude by one device then another. In the final analysis legislative acts became the main devices for collectively enslaving blacks. One such statute reads as follows:

> Be it enacted by the Right Honorable the Lord Proprietary by the advice and consent of the upper and lower house of this present General Assembly, that all Negroes or other slaves already within the province, and all Negro and other slaves to be hereafter imported into the province, shall serve *durante vita*. And all children born of any Negro or other slave shall be slaves as their fathers were, for the term of their lives. And forasmuch as divers freeborn English women, forgetful of their free condition and to the disgrace of our nation, marry Negro slaves, by which also divers suits may arise touching the issue of such women, and a great damage befalls the masters of such Negroes for prevention whereof, for deterring such freeborn women from such shameful matches. Be it further

enacted by the authority, advise, and consent aforesaid, that whatsoever
freeborn woman shall marry any slave from and after the last day of this
present Assembly shall serve the master of such slave during the life of
her husband. And that all the issue of such freeborn women so married
shall be slaves as their fathers were. And be it further enacted, that all the
issue of English or other freeborn women that have already married
Negroes shall serve the masters of their parents till they be thirty years of
age and no longer.[12]

This type of law not only made all blacks slaves but also enslaved
white women who married blacks and their children as well. Sociologically this type of law had four results: first, it enslaved all blacks;
secondly, it made slavery hereditary; third, it barred the children of
freeborn white women from belonging to the white estate of the freeborn; and fourth, it banished from the ranks of the freeborn the white
women who intermarried or mated with black men. And finally, this
type of law effectively precluded any ambiguity concerning racial
origins within the master estate. By this prohibition the master class
could be kept "pure white," and the racial distinctions between masters and servants could be preserved, which would be necessary if the
racial estates were to be maintained over a long period of time.

The only interracial matings that would be permitted would be
extra-legal ones between white men and black women. In these cases,
the white estate was kept racially pure by forcing all offspring of such
mating into the black slave estate, according to the laws of the time
which barred these children from the status of their fathers. A case in
point is the following law:

> Whereas some doubts have arisen whether children got by an English-
> man upon a Negro woman would be slave or free, *be it therefore enacted
> and declared by this present grand assembly*, that all children borne in
> this country shall be held bond or free only according to the condition
> of the mother.[13]

As a result of such laws, all the racially mixed children were relegated to the status of slave. These half-white children became by law
members of the African or Negro "race," and were therefore excluded
from the white estate. Such legal measures kept the white estate, essentially racially pure. By assigning fathers and children different legal
estates, this measure had the effect of removing any legal responsibili-
ties the white fathers might have had for the recognition and mainte-

nance of their half-white children. White men did not have to assume legal recognition of their children, and their children could not legally reckon their lineage by their white fathers. Nor could they inherit their white fathers' statuses or properties. The net result was that the black estate was forced to take responsibility for thousands of abandoned mulatto children whose white fathers did not have to assume legal responsibility for them. These white men also initiated one of the major conditions among blacks: the problem of broken families.

Once established whites had to move to perpetuate this system. Some black servants sought only to live out their terms of servitudes without abolishing the system itself, but laws were instituted to prevent them from purchasing their own freedom. Legislation was passed from time to time to prohibit the voluntary manumission of slaves by benevolent slave owners who wanted to reward some of them for loyal service. Manumission through Christian conversion was also later prohibited by law. One such law read:

> And also it is hereby enacted and declared, . . . That baptism of slaves doth not exempt them from bondage; and that all children shall be bond or free, according to the conditions of their mothers, and the particular directions of this act.[14]

When blacks sought to run away to freedom, the white rulers legislated that runaways were fugitives who could be killed, if necessary, by bounty hunters. A good case in point is the following law:

> Be it enacted . . . that in all such cases upon intelligence of any such negroes, mulattoes or other slaves lying out, two of their majesties justices of the peace of that county . . . shall be impowered and commanded and are hereby impowered and commanded to issue out their warrants directed to the sherrife of the same county to apprehend such negroes, mulattoes, and other slaves, which said sherrife is hereby likewise required upon all such occasions to raise such and soe many forces from time to time as he shall think convenient and necessary for the effectual apprehending such negroes, mulattoes, and other slaves, and in case any negroes, mulattoes or other slaves lying out as aforesaid shall resist, runaway, or refuse to deliver and surrender him or themselves to any person or persons that shall be by lawfull authority employed to apprehend and take such negroes, mulattoes, or other slaves that in such cases it shall and may be lawfull for such person to kill and distroy such negroes, mulattoes and other slaves by gunn or any otherwaise whatsoever.[15]

When slaves ran away more than once, a law permitted them to be branded. Strict punishments were meted out even to those who conspired to help others. When blacks, freed or bound, sought to resist or to defend themselves against white brutality, laws prevented even self-defense. The following was a typical law:

> And if any slave resist his master, or owner, or other person, by his or her order, correcting such slave, and shall happen to be killed in such correction, it shall not be accounted felony; but the master owner, and every such other person so giving correction, shall be free and acquit of all punishment and accusation for the same, as if such accident had never happened: And also, if any negro, mulatto, or Indian, bond or free, shall at any time, lift his or her hand, in opposition against any christian, not being negro, mulatto, or Indian, he or she offending, shall, for every such offence, proved by the oath of the party, receive on his or her bare back, thirty lashes, well laid on; coginizable by a justice of the peace for that county wherein such offence shall be committed.[16]

When black slaves sought to learn an elevated trade, laws were passed to prevent them from learning such work.[17] When they sought education, laws prohibited them from being taught and from learning reading, writing, and arithmetic.[18]

Eventually whites passed laws to prevent blacks from peaceful assembly, free worship, the right to signaling devices or weapons, free speech, free press, and free movement. Some examples appear below:

> *Be it enacted by the authority aforesaid, and it is hereby enacted,* That from henceforth no meetings of negros, or other slaves, be allowed, on any pretence whatsoever, (except as is hereafter excepted.) And that every master, owner, or overseer of any plantation, who shall knowingly or willingly, permit any such meetings, or suffer more than five negros or slaves belonging to his, her, or their plantations or quarters, at any one time, shall forfeit and pay the sum of five shillings, or fifty pounds of tobacco, for each negro or slave, over and above such number, that shall at any time hereafter so unlawfully meet or assemble on his, her, or their plantation, to the informer.[19]
>
> *And be it further enacted, by the authority aforesaid,* That no negro, mulatto, or Indian whatsoever; (except as is hereafter excepted) shall hereafter presume to keep, or carry any gun, powder, shot, or any club, or other weapon whatsoever, offensive or defensive; but that every gun, and all powder and shot, and every such club or weapon, as aforesaid, found or taken in the hands, custody, or possession of any such negro, mulatto, or Indian, shall be taken away; and upon due proof thereof

made, before any justice of the peace of the county where such offence shall be committed, be forfeited to the seisor and informer, and moreover, every such negro, mulatto, or Indian, in whose hands, custody, or possession, the same shall be found, shall, by order of the said justice, have and receive any number of lashes, not exceeding thirty-nine, well laid on, on his or her bare back, for every such offence.[20]

At various times blacks have been prevented by law from owning land, cattle, and material wealth; from buying, selling, and trading; from petitioning, voting, testifying in court, and holding public office. For example:

> *And be it further enacted, by the authority aforesaid, and is hereby enacted and declared,* That no free negro, mulatto, or indian whatsoever, shall hereafter have any vote at the election of burgesses, or any other election whatsoever.[21]

> All negroes, Indians, mulattoes, and all persons of mixed blood, descended from negro and Indian ancestors, to the fourth generation inclusive, (though one ancestor of each generation may have been a white person) whether bond or free, shall be deemed and taken to be incapable in law to be witnesses in any case whatsoever, except against each other.[22]

Efforts to maintain the system extended all the way to beating, torturing, mutilating, maiming, branding, choking, scalding, and applying fire to the back, belly, or genitals. Two samples of such laws follow:

> *Be it enacted,* That where any slave shall hereafter be found notoriously guilty of going abroad in the night, or running away, and lying out, and cannot be reclaimed from such disorderly courses, by the common methods of punishment, it shall and may be lawful, to and for the court of the county, upon complaint and proof thereof to them made, by the owner of such slave, to order and direct every such slave to be punished, by dismembering, or any other way, not touching life, as the said county court shall think fit.[23]

> *Be it enacted,* That where any such Negro, Mulatto, or Indian, shall upon due proof made, or pregnant circumstances appearing before any county court within this colony, be found to have given a false testimony, every such offender shall, without further trial, be ordered by the said court to have one ear nailed to the pillory, and there to stand for the space of one hour, and then the said ear to be cut off; and there after, the other ear nailed in like manner; and cut off, at the expiration of one hour; and

moreover, to order every such offender thirty-nine lashes, well laid on, on his bare back, at the common whipping post.[24]

All whites had the authority, tacit and otherwise, to "correct" all blacks. Unofficial punishments and "corrections" were condoned by the courts. There were few restraints on sadistic racists other than economic ones. Some slaves, no doubt, worked hard to establish their economic worth as protection against involuntary death and excessive brutality. A "good" slave was usually worthy of protection.

For more than a hundred years, blacks have tried to prevent whites from turning them into chattel property. They have invented, conspired, schemed, and fought, but they have not had sufficient power to prevent whites from brutally subjugating them.

Legislation gave legitimacy to all types of subjugation. Many acts of social and economic deprivation were not widely accepted even by whites until the laws coerced them into adherence. These laws made such acts obligatory, uniform, and all-encompassing. Laws ruled out individual prerogative, preferences, and personal arrangements between slaves and masters. Since blacks challenged racism from within and white sympathizers from without, laws were aimed at eliminating all such activities; the law made the maintenance of racism everyone's obligation.

Once the laws were on the books, they had to be enforced, and enforcement came under the domain of the judicial and executive branches of each political jurisdiction. To maintain institutional racism, each branch of government had to be made supportive of it. The courts constituted one of the key instruments of racist power. As such, they were seized like all the other means of control and were used to help perpetuate the system of racial subjugation. The courts could have been used to prevent the institutionalization of the white over the black estate, but in the hands of the racists, they bacame instruments of oppression.

Thus when blacks were not being legislatively stripped of the inalienable constitutional rights of all other Americans, they were litigiously being stripped of these rights through various courts' actions or inactions. The courts were constantly "stacked" with proslavery judges and jurors who repeatedly denied the most elementary human rights to blacks.

Through the years, the racist courts have decided: that blacks were not legal "citizens" and had no rights that whites needed to respect; that blacks were chattel property; that blacks were not entitled to equal protection of the laws; that various land-grant acts did not apply to them; that segregation was constitutional; that blacks could not testify against or sue their white "superiors"; that blacks did not have the legal capacity to choose whether or not they wanted emancipation or slavery.

Dominated by proslavery elements, the courts ruled time and time again against the blacks who petitioned for racial equality. The judiciary upheld the racist laws and added to them with racist decisions and opinions. Petition after petition by blacks and by whites to various legislatures and courts were permitted to die through inaction. The legislatures and courts claimed either that the petitions were not ready for determination, or that they considered the petitions imprudent and premature, or it was advised that citizens who did not possess slaves had better leave the regulation of slavery to those who were cursed with the burden.

As one might suppose, the perpetrators of injustice could hardly be expected to administer justly, and they could hardly be expected to judge themselves and call themselves to task when they were wrong. What was to be expected by these very actions and inactions was that any attempt to dismantle institutionalized racism in any of its forms would be suppressed.

Making the Racial Estates Hereditary

In the United States, interracial mating was extensive between black and white indentured servants and later between freeborn whites and black bondmen. Freed men and women of both races also mated. We have already mentioned that the number of mulatto children in the colonies was notable. However, to establish a society of racial estates, interracial mating had to be curtailed.

Social punishments for interracial mating became institutionalized but some racial mixing continued even when mild social disapproval gave way to harsh legal penalties like public whippings, as in Virginia in 1630. The first legislation punishing interracial marriage and mating was passed in Maryland around 1661.[25] Various colonies at one time or other decreed that white women who mated with blacks would either serve court-appointed masters as slaves, or their children would be slaves until age thirty, or they would be fined or banished from the colony. For example, one Virginia law read:

> *Be it enacted* . . . by the authoritie aforesaid, and it is hereby enacted
> that for the time to come, whatsoever English or other white man or

woman being free shall intermarry with a negro, mullato, or Indian man or woman being free shall within three months after such marriage be banished and removed from this dominion forever. . . . And be it further enacted . . . by the authoritie aforesaid, and it is hereby enacted that if any English woman being free shall have a bastard child by any negro or mullato, she shall pay the sum of fifteen pounds sterling, within one month after such bastard child shall be born, to the Church wardens of the parish where she shall be delivered of such child, and in default of such payment she shall be taken into the possession of the said Church wardens and disposed of for five yeares . . , and the said fine of fifteen pounds, or whatever the woman shall be disposed of for, shall be paid, one third part to their majesties for and towards the support of the government and the contingent charges thereof, and one other third part to the use of the parish where the offence is committed, and the other third part to the informer, and that such bastard child be bound out as a servant by the said Church wardens until he or she shall attaine the age of thirty years, and in case such English woman that shall have such bastard child be a servant, she shall be sold by the said Church wardens, (after her time is expired that she ought by law to serve her master) for five years, and the money she shall be sold for divided as is before appointed, and the child to serve as aforesaid.[26]

Later, in order to prevent the forced enslavement of white women by treacherous white masters, white women who married blacks were freed and their children were also freed, although they were fined and punished in other ways. Some colonies even severely fined clergymen for performing such marriages. For example, in Virginia the law read:

And it be enacted, that no minister of the church of England, or other minister, or person whatsoever, within this colony and dominion, shall hereafter wittingly presume to marry a white man with a negro or mulatto woman; or to marry a white woman with a negro or mulatto man.[27]

White separatism, that is, the maintaining of social and biological separation between blacks and whites, became the cornerstone for maintaining the white estate over the black. Without such social and biological separation, the establishment of racial estates would have fallen before long because of interracial mixing.

White privileges and advantages, based as they were on legal racism, required for their continuance easy ways and means of distinguishing between the dominant and subordinate group members. For this reason, British and American rulers decided quite deliberately

to assign all black-white hybrids to the inferior estate, and any individual who was not "pure white" was defined as "black."

> It is safe to say that in practice one is a Negro or is classed with the
> race if he has the least visible trace of Negro blood in his veins, or even
> if it is known that there was Negro blood in any one of his progenitors.[28]

This irrational and arbitrary decision to assign even those with little
or slight African ancestry to the black race was the extreme to which
white leaders went to maintain the racial purity of the white estate and
the exclusiveness of white advantages and privileges.

> If race distinctions are to be recognized into the law, it is essential that
> the races be clearly distinguished from one another. If a state provides
> that Negroes shall ride in separate coaches and attend separate schools,
> it is necessary to decide first who are included under the term "Negroes."
> It would seem that physical indicia would be sufficient, and in most
> instances, this is true. It is never difficult to distinguish the full-blooded
> Negro, Indian, or Mongolian one from the other or from the Caucasian.
> But the difficulty arises in the blurring of the color line by amalgama-
> tion.[29]
> . . . It is this gradual sloping off from one race into another which has
> made it necessary for the law to set artificial lines.[30]

History has recorded many times that whenever two races have come
into prolonged contact with each other, they have eventually mixed
and mated. Mating has occurred even among those who have defined
the other as ugly and inferior, and no amount of punishment has
prevented other members of the representative racial groups from
mating. When the institutional channels for mating have not existed,
some members of the representative races have mated illicitly. As a
result, there are no "pure" races in the world today.

Perhaps the most interesting question to be drawn from this
situation is: Why do some people try to prevent the members of their
racial groups from mating with others? That is, what purposes does
it serve? The answer lies in the ends of the social institutions. On
rare occasions of inter-racial contact, different racial groups have
wanted to live together in peaceful coexistence, and in these instances,
mating occurred quite permissively. But on most occasions of racial
contact, one race has found it profitable to subjugate and exploit
another race. In doing so, the dominant group has always used the

biological differences to impute "superiority" and "inferiority" to these physiological qualities, and then they have used these imputations as reasons to unequally allocate the scarce social, economic, and political resources and privileges of the society. Accordingly, this has usually meant assigning subjugated people to roles that they have considered inferior, causing the biological marks of the subjugated people to become identified with low status and social degradation. As a corollary, they have always upheld their own biological qualities as symbols of high status and social esteem.

In an attempt to preserve their social, economic, and political advantages, the leaders of the dominant race have had to indoctrinate their members as to their obligations to keep their race biologically pure. The biological purity of the race, as they will often bemoan, is essential for the maintenance of their social, economic, and political privileges, because it is these biological traits which cause their overall superiority. In order that the unearned wealth and privileges be maintained on the basis of race alone, the racial traits of the estates had to be separate and distinct; so racist ideologies were developed to justify white separatism. White separatism made it possible to distinguish between "those who get" and "those who get not."

Those members of the society who would not refrain from interracial mating have usually been subjected to psychological, social, and sometimes even physical abuse. The punishments have ranged from mild social disapproval to whippings, excommunication, prison sentences, and sentences to servitude and slavery. Such punishments have been applied to men, women, and children in attempts to stop racial mixing. The ultimate end of such harsh punishments in a multiracial society is racial privilege. Permissive mating would have eventually blurred the racial distinctions of the races and would have erased the bases for racially defined privileges. Thus the races had to be kept biologically separate in order to maintain the estate and caste relations. Biological amalgamation would have destroyed the dominant and subordinate relationships between the races for without clear racial differences and without a basis of racial discrimination, privileges could be neither consistently applied nor biologically justified.

Since interracial mating, regardless of punishment, could never be completely prevented, multi-racial societies have had to make arrangements for the racially hybrid children who would eventually appear. Attempts to institutionalize middle castes or middle estates of racial hybrids have not been successful. To solve the problem of hybrids, the dominant race usually has defined the hybrid as a subracial or subcolor category of the subordinate peoples, and such individuals were required to suffer the same deprivations and restrictions as the members of the subordinate estate and caste. The biological marks inherited from the subordinate race become in their cases the quick and lasting marks of a stigmatized social origin. Being neither fully recognizable as one race nor the other, some hybrids have had the biological capability of "passing" for more than one race. In closed and racially stratified societies, racially mixed people have almost always wanted to identify with the dominant group's status and privileges when they were able. But, in such societies, the dominant race usually has resisted full acceptance of such hybrids as part of their group, and has therefore been reluctant to extent the social privileges and other advantages even to hybrids who have only a "taint" of the inferior racial marks about them. To extend these privileges to hybrids would have eroded the unearned privileges which the dominant group exclusively enjoyed—the essential point of racial discrimination. The stigma attached to racial hybrids has forced some of them to choose to "pass" as members of the dominant or a foreign race.

Race-by-Ancestry: The Reality

The colonial society became based on racial ancestry, wherein race had become an imposed social convention rather than a biological concept.

> The "Negro race" is defined in America by the white people. Everybody having a known trace of Negro blood—no matter how far back it was acquired—is classified as a Negro. No amount of white ancestry, except one hundred percent, will permit entrance to the white race.[31]
>
> This social definition of the Negro race, even if it does not change anything in the biological situation, increases the number of individuals included in the Negro race. It relegates a large number of individuals who look like white people, or almost so, to the Negro race.[32]

Using ancestry rather than appearance, the dominant group's leaders instituted a rigid system of race classification. Ancestry is something one cannot change, so privileges and rights decreed on the basis of ancestry are equally unchangeable. Under this system those who were fully Caucasian in appearance, but who were known to have a trace of African ancestry were still "black," as the dominant group had decreed. But the system did not pertain in reverse; that is to say, being African in appearance but having white ancestry did not make one "white." By relegating all mixed-blood people to the subordinated group, the system discouraged intermarriage. It discouraged dominant-group initiatives toward intermarriage, for white skin, blue eyes, blond hair, and sharp facial features would not in and of themselves qualify their children to be members of the white race in the system of race-by-ancestry.[33] Ancestry, regardless of appearance, was the ultimate test.

Ignoring appearances and basing all rights and privileges on racial origin, the system of race relationships became very rigid. Once different sociopolitical roles and different social privileges were assigned by racial ancestry, the social order was set for generations since ancestry could not be changed nor easily denied. A key reason for prohibiting intermarriage between the races was to maintain racial privileges, and since race-by-ancestry was such an immutable criterion, using it the dominant group was able to build a rigid social system of white over black.·

To maintain the race-by-ancestry system whites had to institute prohibition on social integration and biological amalgamation. If a substantial number of family members like uncles, aunts, grandparents, cousins, and in-laws became mixed through intermarriage, rigid social segregation by race could not be easily maintained. The violence and repression used to subordinate those of the black estate could not have been used if sympathetic revulsion by white loved ones occurred. Thus, white separatism became a sociological imperative for maintaining white supremacy.

In the system of race-by-ancestry all individuals of known African ancestry, whether they appeared to be white, or were obviously black, suffered the same social and economic deprivations as a result of their common estate designation. Race-by-ancestry therefore caused some "near-white" individuals to suffer lasting and extreme forms of social degradation and perpetual economic servitude as a result of legal-political rules separating "pure" white and "near-white" people. The polity not biology caused them to live and marry as orders of human beings separated from their white relatives. Visible and immutable traits of African ancestry became signs allowing whites to practice rigid and lasting racial discrimination against those people who were genotypically white.

Interestingly enough these very legal-political estates became bases
of coalition politics. Both pure blacks and near-whites of the black
estate have organized sometimes secretly and sometimes not so secretly according to their common interests, common sentiments of opposition, and common strategies, all inherent in their common legal-
political position. Collective "antiblack" discrimination and prejudice invariably have led to a consciousness of collective problems
among those of African descent. Being already forced together by
official policies of segregation, avoidance, and exclusion, blacks and
near-whites had only to bring themselves together to insulate themselves from demoralizing attacks by whites. Coming together, they
eventually developed several racial ideologies, along with several
protest strategies. They even formed protest organizations in order to
protect themselves from harm, and in order to eliminate the discriminatory racial practices which restricted their rights, their social
advancement, and their economic betterment. This type of coalition
between blacks and near-whites was inherent in the race-by-ancestry
system.

Collective racial repression always begets collective racial consciousness, and that consciousness always begets collective racial struggle.
Because whites, through the race-by-ancestry system, excluded all of
those of African descent from high-level occupations, political enfranchisement, religious dignity, educational attainment, and family
integrity, the blacks were emotionally moved to conspire against the
dominant group's racist practices. In doing so, they worked out three
basic orientations and modes of action. One mode was to gain some
effective influence within the political, economic, and social institutions. The second mode was to develop community institutions to
the point where separation from the dominant group might be feasible.
The third mode was to develop strength enough to repel the attacks
of the dominant group and then to move offensively against the white
racists' legal, political, economic, and social institutions.

Race-by-ancestry is our cultural heritage from the colonial days,
and the black-white conflict today is a natural and predictable dialectic of that type of social system.

Race-by-Appearance: The Hypothetical Alternative
Extensive biological amalgamation of whites and blacks would have
produced a different system of race relations. It would have produced
a system of race-by-appearance. Amalgamation would have so mixed

the races that discrimination by ancestry eventually would have been impossible. Since the racial origins would have been so mixed within families, discrimination by ancestry would have caused division in the families of the dominant group.

In a system of race-by-appearance, those individuals having Caucasian-like skin color, hair texture, and facial features would have been considered "whites" regardless of whether their grandparents, cousins, brothers, or sisters were designated as "blacks." In a system of race-by-appearance, the racial labels "black" and "white" would only *describe* racial appearance—skin color, hair texture, and facial features, and since racial terms would be only descriptions of appearances, not origins, blacks and whites could belong to the same families, and of course to the same social clubs, without racial discrimination.

The society would have been so racially mixed that even those persons with racist inclinations would not have been able to segregate themselves racially into clear-cut social groups of blacks and whites. With extensive amalgamation, there would have come into existence several racially mixed biological types varying from pure black to pure white.

In Puerto Rico, a well-amalgamated society, whoever is not black is some variation of the Caucasian race. Hybrids predominate and are categorized into several different sociobiological categories, namely, Blancos, Tregueños, Indios, Grifos, and Negroes, according to their appearances. These sociobiological designations carry no restrictions on participation in economic, political, or social institutions.

Accordingly, in a system of race-by-appearance, blacks would not necessarily have been forced into predetermined inferior roles rationed only to those of Negroid appearance. Having a Negroid racial appearance would not have condemned one to immutable social stagnation. Blacks, accordingly, would have been neither limited by legal requirements nor subordinated to whites. Neither would blacks have had their educational and political efforts nullified by race restrictions. It is obvious that if sociopolitical curtailments had been legislated using racial appearances as bases of race distinctions, families would have been split: husbands from wives, brothers from sisters, grandparents from grandchildren, and cousins from cousins. The foundation of society, the family, would have been destroyed.

In summary, great racial amalgamation would have left the colonial population with such a mixture of racial features that there would have been no basis for consistent racial segregation. As long as intermixing occurred between all racial types (shades and features), racial equality would have been assured, for the individuals in society would have appeared different only in degrees, not in kind. Racial legislation would have been socially destructive in a society where most people would have had some Caucasian and some Negroid features. Any legislation which discriminated according to racial features to determine where each racial category would live, sleep, eat, drink, study, sit, or marry would not have worked among the citizens in a well-amalgamated society.

As a consequence, and perhaps most importantly, those of different racial designations would not have been forced to develop a racial self-consciousness and a political consciousness of separate socio-political interests. There would have been no common need for "racial" solidarity. [Such a society would not even have developed racial protest organizations.] Family identification would have been stronger than racial identification, and class consciousness would have been even more developed than racial consciousness. Family and class origins, not racial origins, would have been the chief bases for determining social and sexual intercourse. Consequently, there would have emerged no felt needs for organizations like the NAACP, CORE, or the Black Muslims. Since neither legal repression nor discrimination by race would have been practiced, no racial protest movements would have developed. The labels "white" and "black" would have been only descriptive terms not prescriptive terms. If "racial" discrimination existed at all, it would have been a matter of individual preference. Personal prejudice exercised simultaneously and collectively could have given rise to collective group reactions on the part of those discriminated against, but with so much racial mixture and so much variation in appearance in each extended family, such unanimity in personal prejudice inevitably would have caused division in the family. Any such collective prejudice would have been short-lived because family unity would have militated against racism within family circles and hence within the society at large.

Passing: Race-by-Ancestry versus Race-by-Appearance

In a racist society, some blacks have felt moved and pressured to deny their African heritage. They have tried to claim that they had ancestors of some other group. This phenomenon is called "passing," and it has been a pathway to better jobs, better homes, and better social treatment. Because of these opportunities for betterment, some light-complexioned Afro-Americans have tried to convert themselves into "Creoles," "Indians," "Puerto Ricans," or "West Indians." Some dark-complexioned Afro-Americans have tried to become "Indians," "Arabs," and "Cubans."

These passers—"Cubans," "West Indians," "Creoles," "Indians," and "whites"—have lived as marginal persons on the fringes of either the ethnic or the black community. They have been called "marginal persons" because they have had to live apart from the two main racial groups and thus have participated incompletely in both communities.

Some of these individuals have tried to acquire special legal recognition of their heritages, but whites have not recognized them as separate from other blacks. Regardless of what passers have called themselves, most whites have not desired intimate association with them. Those Afro-Americans who have fully identified themselves as such have also disliked attempts by these self-styled blacks to acquire for themselves a recognition of an ancestral status superior to that of the Afro-American.

In a race-by-ancestry system, light-complexioned persons and dark-complexioned persons commonly belong to the same black family. Therefore, considerable strain emerges when some members choose to claim an ethnic origin different from that of the family. By doing so, in order to acquire social advantages different from those of the other family members, these individuals arouse great hostility.

Those engaging in this "game" of race-by-identity have had no legal means to segregate themselves socially from other non-whites. They have been so poorly organized and powerless in American society that they have lived almost unnoticed on the fringes of the black community. In periods of great racial polarization, however, many of them have had to "close ranks," and return to the black community as Afro-Americans.

On the other hand, in the system of race-by-ancestry, light-complexioned Afro-Americans who have identified themselves unconditionally as Afro-Americans have often achieved high economic positions in the black community. They have been so successful because they have been physically more acceptable to white employers, given the latter's prejudices of color and origin. Light-complexioned Afro-Americans have usually been the first ones permitted by whites to integrate economically and socially. This degree of discrimination-by-appearance has caused conflicts between light and dark blacks, confusing them as to whether the operative system is one of discrimination-by-origin, or discrimination-by-appearance. The truth is that both operate to some degree, but the former takes priority over the latter when conflicts arise.

2 White Strategies

Legal-political Strategies

Exploitation, segregation, and subordination of blacks have been the major ends pursued and perpetuated legislatively and litigiously by whites for three hundred years. Laws of almost every conceivable kind have been enacted to achieve these three ends. Legislatures and courts have resisted virtually every attempt by blacks either to change the system, to abolish it, or to advance themselves within it.

Blacks, both freed and bound, have sought to prevent the institutionalization of racial inequality from the beginning, but they have always been outnumbered, and number meant power in the early days. Through the years, they have struggled to reverse the legislative and court decisions which legalized racial exploitation, but whites issued still more laws and decisions to prevent these liberation efforts. Blacks have sought to get new laws passed through the legislative process, but whites used social measures like terror to suppress these efforts.

These whites who did not wish to support slavery and other forms of racism were also legislatively and judicially coerced into supporting the racists. As was pointed out in Chapter One, many laws were passed to coerce white resisters into compliance. Freeborn white men and women of the anti-slavery persuasion found themselves reluctantly supporting the immorality of slavery under penalty of law. The more they have challenged the system, the more measures were taken to suppress their resistance. The laws required that all whites maintain the racial order. The slave-treatment codes inscribed in laws were binding on antiracists as well as on black slaves.

We have already documented the fact that the white rulers and advocates of institutional racism deliberately set on a course to create a white-dominated society with racial discrimination as an organizing principle. Later, when they needed a forced-labor class, they found black laborers most easily identifiable, and most clearly indefensible. It should be noted that slavery could not have been so rigid and lasting without legal shackles. Slavery could not have had the wide spread support it did without being supported by officials of the state. The political leaders used the legislative and litigatory processes to generalize, routinize, and institutionalize what already were the customary practices of a small number. Legislation forced conformity to slavery and gave moral credibility to a practice supposedly abhorred by most early settlers of the colonies.

The enslavement of a whole race was not only a legal act, but an act against the nature of man as well. The inferiority of a whole race of people has never occurred and could never occur simply by biological traits alone, so legal-political measures had to be devised to fulfill this racist dream. Whites had to use a system of legal-political controls to suppress the real innate abilities and potentialities of blacks. One of the first controls was indoctrination.

Indoctrination

The slave owners found it expedient to use religious instruction to control the minds and imaginations of blacks.[1] The first preachers were whites, who told blacks that they had a moral duty to be obedient slaves and that they would get their rewards in heaven if they persevered. The preachers also taught them that if whites wronged them, God and only God could punish them in the Judgment. Later, black preachers encouraged black redemptive suffering, as illustrated in these words:

> Violence is the argument of cowards and unwise people. Shotguns correct nothing. Swords conquer nothing. Those who use the sword must perish by it. The Negro has the most powerful weapon known among men. It is the only convincing argument. It is the only weapon which brings lasting conquest. It is the sword of the spirit. It is faith in God. The Negro cannot hope to succeed with carnal armament. But with spirit forces there is no ocean which he cannot cross, no Alps which he cannot scale. Persecutions in time turn on the persecutor with a thousandfold

more destructive malignity than were visited upon the persecuted. Wrongs are like the boomerang and return to the one who hurls them with more deadly results than they inflicted upon the intended victim. No people were ever persecuted down. They were always persecuted up.[2]

The black masses were told that God had a plan in enslaving them. Many preachers also told them that their suffering, no matter how unjust, would turn to greater glory in the future:

> Nothing is immortal but mind. Nothing survives but spirit. Nothing triumphs but soul. The Jewish people are the fittest people in the annals of man. They alone live. All others die. All nations, whether ancient or modern, have been broken and shattered in proportion to the intensity with which they have thrown themselves against this spiritual people. Oppress them, they increase. Persecute them, they flourish. Discriminate against them, they grow rich. They go right on growing stronger by the cruelty of their enemies. Babylon carried them into captivity. The Jew is here. Where is Babylon? Egypt has beat him with many stripes while he built her pyramids, her sphinx, and her gigantic lake. The Jew is here, the pyramids and sphinx which he built are here. Where is Egypt? Rome whipped the Colosseum out of his muscles. The Colosseum is here. The Jew is here. Where is bloody Rome? Such will be the history of spiritual races unto the end. The Negro is a spiritual race.[3]

Whites also encouraged blacks to believe in a "this-worldly" philosophy of redemptive suffering which went as follows: if blacks could develop the capacity to endure more suffering than the oppressors could inflict on them, the white oppressors would eventually see the brutality of their ways; they would eventually see themselves as wrongdoers and, through self-reflection on these brutalities would come to feel guilt, remorse, and revulsion concerning their own inhumanity to blacks. Through this self-reflection and conversion, black suffering could become redemptive in this world too.

Many others, however, among them black abolitionists and black preachers, did not accept this philosophy. Their view is reflected in the following excerpt:

> To SUCH DEGRADATION IT IS SINFUL IN THE EXTREME FOR YOU TO MAKE VOLUNTARY SUBMISSION. The divine commandments you are in duty bound to reverence and obey. If you do not obey them, you will surely meet with the displeasure of the Almighty. He requires you to love him supremely, and your neighbor as yourself—to

keep the Sabbath day holy—to search the Scriptures—and bring up your children with respect for his laws, and to worship no other God but him. But slavery sets all these at nought, and hurls defiance in the face of Jehovah. The forlorn condition in which you are placed does not destroy your moral obligation to God. You are not certain of heaven, because you suffer yourselves to remain in a state of slavery, where you cannot obey the commandments of the Sovereign of the universe. If the ignorance of slavery is a passport to heaven, then it is a blessing, and no curse, and you should rather desire its perpetuity than its abolition. God will not receive slavery, nor ignorance, nor any state of mind, for love and obedience to him. Your condition does not absolve you from your moral obligation. The diabolical injustice by which your liberties are cloven down, *NEITHER GOD, NOR ANGELS, NOR JUST MEN, COMMAND YOU TO SUFFER FOR A SINGLE MOMENT. THERE-FORE IT IS YOUR SOLEMN AND IMPERATIVE DUTY TO USE EVERY MEANS, MORAL, INTELLECTUAL, AND PHYSICAL, THAT PROMISES SUCCESS.* If a band of heathen men should attempt to enslave a race of Christians and to place their children under the influence of some false religion, surely Heaven would frown upon the men who would not resist such aggression, even to death. If, on the other hand, a band of Christians should attempt to enslave a race of heathen men, and to entail slavery upon them, and to keep them in heathenism in the midst of Christianity, the God of Heaven would smile upon every effort which the injured might make to disenthral themselves.[4]

When their brainwashing and indoctrination did not work, the white slaveholders devised other methods of control. One device was to use the sympathetic natural "leaders" within the slave community to lead the black masses in accordance with the wishes of the masters.

Indirect Rule

The technique of indirect rule involved controlling the black masses through intermediaries who acted as the leaders of the group. By controlling the black leaders, the hands of the oppressor worked invisibly and indirectly behind the scenes instead of visibly and directly.[5]

Over the years, the black leaders have been overseers, drivers, team leaders, preachers, politicians, or bureaucrats. They have functioned in essentially two ways: to communicate the directives of the white superiors to the black masses in acceptable terms, and to act as monitors of the group activities.

The most conspicuous agents of the white oppressors through the years have been the black preachers. Preachers have been able to hold positions of prestige and privilege among whites in proportion to their ability to control the black masses. Their chief devices of control were indoctrination (discussed in the preceding section) and sponsorship. Sponsorship worked in this manner: Those black followers who did not threaten to overthrow the institutional system, which the preachers were pledged to maintain, were rewarded by being "sponsored" by these black preachers when opportunities for better jobs or for certain privileges were provided by the white leaders.

At times when black leaders were delegated powers to make decisions, some of them assumed the same social and psychological posture as that of the dominant group's leaders; in doing so, they became just as hostile, just as negative, just as bigoted, and just as cruel as their white masters. This was indirect rule at its best.

Divide and Rule: The Spy System

Within the slave estate, there was a hierarchy of privileged orders. The first order was that of personal servants; the second, household servants; the third, drivers; and the fourth, field workers. These various slave categories were pitted against one another in order to keep blacks in disunity.[6] House slaves were most commonly pitted against field slaves, and betrayals of fellow slaves were well rewarded. Freedom was often granted for "meritorious service," which was equivalent to saving the lives and properties of white masters from destruction by informing about slave revolts and conspiracies.

Some blacks were full-time undercover spies of their white masters; that is, they were full-time traitors. The mulatto house slaves, especially, were frequently recruited for the task of spying, and they revealed more slave revolt plots than any other group. They also, more than others, reported thefts, runaways, and other acts of liberation by black slaves, especially acts by field slaves. Sociologically this situation is understandable. The house slaves were often the half-white offspring of the master himself. They closely identified with their masters, who in turn gave their offspring special privileges. Playing on the mulatto slaves' desires to be counted among the superior human beings, masters encouraged them to prove their loyalty and worth by protecting the master and his family against pernicious acts by rebellious blacks.

Whites encouraged many hybrids to regard themselves as biologically superior by virtue of their "white blood." Socially, they gave them the best jobs, the best opportunities for education, and the best clothes and privileges. They became a color class within the black estate. In defending their class advantages, they at times defended the master's interests. This was divide and rule at its best.

Police and Paramilitary Controls

The cities of the South used mostly private guards, military soldiers, and municipal police. The rural areas used citizen patrols and citizen vigilantes.[7] Blacks feared these patrols because they raided the cabins, homes, and gathering places of Blacks to interrogate "suspicious" blacks. They searched out and broke up "unapproved" meetings of blacks, and applied "correction" to blacks who were not conforming to the doctrine of black servility.

White youths were drafted for service in these patrols much as youths have been subject to the military draft in this century. To fully control slaves, constant police presence was necessary. Some foreign visitors to the South thought that all southern white men were soldiers or policemen. Militias of all kinds—local, state, and national —were needed to put down frequent insurrections by blacks. Whites in the South lived, it seems, in something approximating a police state. For this reason, many non-slaveholding whites advocated the abolition of slavery. The fears of such whites encouraged the abolition of the slave system, through the antislavery movements.

According to Wade, the cities required more stringent and more aggressive surveillance than did the countryside because of the density of the black population, their close social mingling, and their greater freedom of movement and therefore of action in the urban areas. This relative freedom necessitated the constant presence of white policing to keep blacks "in their place."

To complement the patrol system, blacks had to carry identification cards (passes) which specified the slaves' owners, their reasons for being away from their masters' premises, and the items which they should have in their possession. Free blacks also had to carry such cards in order to prove they were not runaway slaves. If they had no such cards, they could be reenslaved—and many were.

In times of serious insurrection, volunteer "companies" of white men were formed from various parts of the region. They were given the authority to protect white lives and property at any cost and to apply "correction" to insubordinate blacks. These patrols were the obvious progenitors of the Ku Klux Klan.

The dominant group did not stop with organized militias. Physical devices for slave control were devised to complement the patrols. Iron shackles, whips, branding irons, treadmills, workhouses, and pillories were all used to keep the blacks under control. Extensive controls in one form or another were always present, and their existence gave the lie to the white contention that the slaves were happy, compliant and well treated.

Terrorism

The dominant group was willing to use any means necessary including terrorism to maintain institutional racism. Gestapo tactics, vigilante tactics, and lynch-mob rule were frequently used against blacks, both freed and enslaved. Free blacks were also kept "in their place" largely through terrorist tactics by white mobs who were granted official immunity from persecution if they broke the law in the process of applying "corrections" to blacks. Mutilations, lynchings, assassinations, pogroms, and other tactics were used and were supported by judicial and political leaders.

The most infamous organized terrorism was perpetrated by the Ku Klux Klan.[8] The group was formed in Tennessee by General Nathan Forrest.

> The original "Invisible Empire" was organized by Confederate Veterans in 1866 and shrank neither from intimidation nor from violence in a successful effort to prevent former slaves from exercising their recently acquired political and economic rights.[9]

After the Civil War, the Klan took it upon itself to maintain the white-over-black system when the legislatures and the courts no longer openly supported and sanctioned it. White citizens, mostly from the lower classes, were recruited by the Klan as vigilante terrorists. Many nonmembers gave sometimes tacit and sometimes open approval to their activities, and white leaders also protected them through the courts and through the communication media when the Klansmen's wrongdoings became public. These KKK terrorists became so powerful that they "ruled" not only blacks but also reluctant whites who did not condone black repression. The Klan consistently used arson, beatings, murder, and tarring-and-feathering as terror tactics. Since its beginning, the Klan has been responsible for thousands of known deaths and perhaps tens of thousands of untold deaths of both blacks and whites.

Indirect Disfranchisement

The electoral system too has been used in black suppression.[10]

Various political devices have been invented and put into practice, the most famous of which has been the white primary. Only whites were permitted to vote in primary elections, and thus only whites could nominate candidates for various offices. Since primaries determined the ultimate outcomes in the general elections, blacks were effectively excluded from influencing the election of government leaders.

A second device was the poll tax. According to the law, blacks were required to pay a tax before voting. But since the poll taxes were annually cumulative, blacks who had not been able to vote during the previous years had to pay all the accumulated taxes before voting. Many blacks could afford to pay only the initial tax assessment, and not the cumulated assessments, and they were kept from voting.

A third device was the literacy test. Blacks had to demonstrate to registrars that they were literate enough to vote intelligently. The registrars were always white, and they almost always failed blacks regardless of formal preparation. Black college graduates were examined by near-illiterate white registrars and were failed. The system allowed personal prejudice, whim, and caprice to enter into the voter-registration process, and as a result blacks had virtually no chance of meeting the voting requirements. When blacks could pass the literacy tests, the registration applications would "run out." If they were able to fill out registration cards, their names were subsequently "lost" or "accidentally" left off the list of registered voters. When black voters did manage to overcome all of these contrivances, whites would redraw the geographic boundaries so as to split up the concentrations of black voters. Thus gerrymandering also nullified the effect of voting.

Administrative Denial of Civil Rights[11]

The administrative devices to deprive blacks of their civil rights have most commonly taken the form of (1) obstructionism, (2) gradualism, (3) nullification, and (4) unequal application of the laws.

One very popular administrative tactic has been obstructionism—that is, delay for its own sake. Legislative and litigious processes are slow enough without deliberate delays, but such processes can be further delayed. Legislative and litigious indecision at a time when the denial of someone's civil rights is the principal effect, is obstructionism. Filibusters, arbitrary committee actions, postponements of decisions, and denial of expeditious enforcement of laws are examples of obstructionist actions regularly used against blacks.

The second administrative tactic, gradualism, is the slow, piecemeal granting of overdue legal rights. The gradual state-by-state and law-by-law of granting of overdue civil rights invites protest movements to speed up the process, because justice delayed is justice denied.

Nullification, the third administrative tactic, prohibits the enjoyment of civil rights granted by law. Nullification has been accomplished either by (1) the withholding of official protection from those who wish to exercise their rights, or by (2) the prosecuting on unfounded criminal charges of those who do exercise their rights. A case in point was the exposure of black freedom fighters to the mobs and assassins after the blacks had been taken into official custody. As official protection was not forthcoming, lynch-mob law was permitted to operate. Assault, arson, maiming, and other mob actions were visited upon black freedom fighters who were already in the custody of white officials. Another example of nullification in operation was the arrest of blacks who sought to be served at customarily segregated lunch counters. Many were charged with "inciting to riot."

The fourth administrative tactic is unequal application of the laws. White judges commonly mete out unequal punishments for black and white criminals found guilty of the same crime; blacks who perpetrate crimes against whites are penalized more severely. Equal protection of the laws is nonexistent in such cases.

The historical record indicates that administrative trickery has been commonly used against blacks. Courts, in sum, have cheated blacks, denied blacks, ruled against blacks, oversentenced blacks, and granted judicial immunity to white perpetrators of violence against blacks. This pattern of administrative repression has had the same ultimate end as all other forms of repression—to keep blacks "in their place."

Economic Strategies

Chattel Slavery

Slavery was essentially an economic system, supported at its foundation by political despotism. As a system of production, it existed side by side with the system of contract labor and the system of free wage labor. Contrary to popular belief, the white capitalists had several labor systems in operation at the same time. Why did black chattel slavery come to predominate? The answer lies in profit maximization and in political despotism. The capitalists, searching for ways to maximize profits, needed cheap labor as the most efficient means to achieve this end. Labor was, and still is, the most costly factor in production; thus, it is not surprising that capitalists would be attracted to the cheapest labor available.

> Slavery was essentially a labor system designed to meet the opportunities for the development of the New World. Free white laborers were scarce and they were unwilling to work in hot, sickly climates as agricultural workers when cheap land was available. As whites proved intractable, African labor was enslaved. The effectiveness of this slave labor system depended upon the economic aggressiveness and managerial efficiency of masters and overseers.[12]

Clearly then, slavery in the American colonies was not a domestic slavery but a capitalistic slavery. Capitalistic slavery is characterized by large landholdings with large numbers of unfree laborers who are organized and coordinated in a systematic way to produce a commercial staple crop. Most slaves in the American colonies and states worked under such conditions on large plantations. Only 12 percent of the planters held more than 50 percent of all the slaves. These same large planters became so commercially oriented that they often raised a breeding stock for the single purpose of maintaining their own stock of slaves.

The capitalistic nature of the system of slavery is revealed in the connections of the planters with the financial capital of the time. Southern banks were heavily involved in plantation capitalism.

> Southern banks were primarily designed to lend the planters money for outlays that were economically feasible and socially acceptable in a slave society: the movement of crops, the purchases of land and slaves, and little else.[13]

The profitability of slavery was its chief reason for existence. Although there is much disagreement about whether or not the cost of purchasing a slave and maintaining him was equivalent to the cost of a free worker's wage bill, the majority would agree that in most areas, during most of the years of slavery, and especially on big plantations, the cost of maintaining a slave was smaller than the free worker's bill, even though the productivity of the free worker was greater. The fact that slavery survived for hundreds of years, and the fact that many planters amassed great fortunes under this system of commerce, are sufficient reasons for concluding that slave labor was profitable, even though perhaps more costly than other systems of labor. This latter contention has not yet been proved by historians or political economists.

Because of the commercial nature of slavery, the black slave was, for all intents and purposes, reduced to the status of a beast of burden. On most large plantations, the slaves were branded like cattle, "broken in," and trained. The way to high profits was to keep the stock, human and nonhuman, in good health and in working order. For this reason persuasion, bribery, cajolery, manipulation, and other types of nonviolent inducements were used more often than whipping, shackling, maiming, and confining to a lockup. There was a widespread belief that slaves could not be made to work well with cruel punishments; so loyalty, pride, and prospect of reward were constantly advocated in the treatment of slaves.

> Whippings, instead of proving a cure, might bring revenge in the form of sabotage, arson or murder. Adequacy in food, clothing and shelter might prove of no avail, for contentment must be mental as well as physical. The preventives mainly relied upon were holidays, gifts and festivities to create lightness of heart; overtime and overtask payments to promote zeal and satisfaction; kindliness and care to call forth loyalty in return; and the special device of crop patches to give every hand a stake in the plantation.[14]

High profits were contingent upon reducing production costs. As a result, slaves were given only subsistence provisions and no more. When slaves planted crops on their patches in sufficient quantities to sell some for income, the income went to the masters, who issued tickets for merchandise which the slaves could pick up at the commissary. The main provisions supplied by masters were salt pork, molasses, coffee, corn meal, salt, and sugar. Vegetables and other provisions the slave had to grow himself on his own time if he wanted anything more than the basics.

The slaves were provided with clapboard cabins which were whitewashed inside and out from time to time. Furniture was almost non-existent. They slept on mattresses stuffed with fresh hay or corn shucks. Every spring and fall the houses were emptied and cleaned out, and the contents brought outside to be aired. Near the cabins were small patches for growing subsistence crops.

The slaves usually received clothes twice a year. The quantities varied according to the master and the economic conditions. Typically, the men were given a couple of shirts and pairs of trousers twice a year. The women got cloth, needles, thread, and buttons to make their own clothes, or they were given shifts, frocks, and sacks.

The object of all care and feeding of slaves was profit. Slave labor was the most important factor of production, and great concern surrounded the care and treatment of slaves. Slavery was basically a production system. The masters were very attentive to maintenance and supervision costs, amortization of capital investments, and insurance against premature death, illness, old age, and taxes. Blacks were treated as working stock. They were bred, fed, and raised with an eye to profits. It was planned that by the time a slave reached his teens, his earning would gradually cover all of his current charges, including his supervision.

> A slave's highest rate of earning would be reached of course when his physical maturity and his training became complete, and would normally continue until his bodily powers began to flag.[15]

Blacks were valued as property from the point of view of profits. Slave owners were constantly appraising the ratio between the annual net earnings of a slave, and his capital value.

> At the age of twenty it might well be as ten to one; at the age of fifty it would probably not exceed four to one; at sixty-five it might be less than a parity.[16]

A slave's value was affected by age, sex, physique, training, mental agility, and moral qualities. All else being equal, blacks were often valued in accordance with the price of cotton. If cotton was worth twelve cents a pound, a black male in his prime might be worth $1,200; if cotton was fifteen cents a pound, the male was worth $1,500.[14]

Slavery was a business system, but it gave rise to a style of life which complemented the business relationships. The plantation itself became more than an agribusiness. A whole etiquette of human relationships evolved to regulate the social relationships among the slaves and between the slaves and the masters. The day-to-day existence of the slaves, the marriage patterns, the child-rearing patterns, the recreational forms, the lack of social and political participation in the community were all complements of the economic arrangements and were made permanent by the political machinations of the white power structure. Since the free wage-labor system, the contract wage-labor system, and the serfdom-labor system were all operating at the same time to some degree, one could conclude that the chattel-slave system which, eventually became predominant in the South was forged and erected not only by market forces but also by political forces which were encouraged by political motives to maximize political power over the masses.

Debt Peonage

As slavery ended, blacks were forced into another kind of servitude. Black servitude was reinstituted in the form of debt peonage. Freed without land or financial reparations, the black ex-slaves were forced into indebtedness to the large landowners. Through high interest rates and high prices for commodities the owners insured black indebtedness. As they became tied financially to the landowners, the owners gained control over the means of relieving indebtedness; practically, blacks became indentured servants again.

Vagrancy laws and criminal laws were used to bind those blacks who would not bind themselves voluntarily. For example, blacks who appeared idle on the streets were rounded up and hustled to court as vagrants. Thier fines were paid by landowners who needed cheap labor, and the court would turn the blacks over to the landowners to work out their fines—hence forced labor through judicial decision.

The debt-peonage system was a "natural" outgrowth of the system of indentured servitude and chattel slavery. When black unfree labor was set free by law, whites needed to bind it by other means. These other means became economic and sociopolitical:

> The sharecropper is an agricultural worker who has only his labor to sell. He may work on a large plantation of five, ten, twenty or thirty thousand acres, or he may work on a small farm. His landlord may hire him directly or he may hire himself to a planter who rents the land from a landlord who rents the land from a real estate dealer in Kansas City who leases it for a syndicate in New York and whose members may be scattered over half the world. Thus on the back of one man four or five others may be living in luxury while he himself toils and sweats usually for his keep, or as Norman Thomas has so aptly said, "he farms for exercise."

Black workers had to be subdued, immobilized, and contained after emancipation, and indebtedness was the main mechanism for doing all three. This economic system was backed up politically with one-sided laws and one-sided law enforcers who themselves were paid agents of the landowners. The landowners' foremen and overseers became sheriff's deputies during the pursuit of idle laborers and runaway tenants. In this way law enforcers were obliged to work in the interests of the landowners.

The debt-peonage system is one in which a debtor must work out in compulsory service what he owes to his creditor. The sharecropper becomes a peon, or debtor, to the planter when the latter furnishes provisions to the sharecropper on which to live for the duration of the growing and harvesting season. A tenant-farmer/sharecropper, in order to get seeds and supplies to raise the first crop, therefore had to go into debt in order to feed himself and his family. He remained in debt because his share of the profits at the end of the season hardly ever equaled the debt, which was made artificially high and out of reach by exploitatively high interest rates and high prices for provisions. More important than the high interest rates was the employers' *undisputed* control over all financial accounts. It has been claimed that most employers were dishonest and that they got rich by fraudulent manipulation of the books and other such devices.

> . . . The planter "keeps books" and is "always careful that no laborer exceeds his account," and makes "sure that at the end of the year he (the planter) has gotten it all, and his labor has just lived." The sharecropper keeps no accounts, no books; it is useless to do so. When the little slip of paper is handed him bearing figures in black and red he makes no comments, asks no questions. He just looks at them, talks about them to his neighbors, goes home to his wife, dejected, downhearted, hopeless. Another year has come and gone; he has worked hard—hard as a slave—and what has he now? Nothing but a slip of paper with little figures in black and red. Another year of grinding toil faces him; maybe he will do better next year. There is hope for a while, but not for long, for he knows deep down in his heart that the future is hopeless. A great loneliness and despair seize him, and he sits down and with hands grown large from heavy work brushes away tears from eyes glued to the cotton stalks in his doorway.[19]

It was the plantation owners who marketed the crops at the end of the season. Accordingly, they were in a position to take whatever share they felt covered the "advances" which they had made. They also dictated the prices, the interests, the shares, the profits, and even the quota of the next year's crop. They determined the seeds to be planted, the subsistence crops to be raised, the diet provided, the degree of indebtedness, and the length of time allowed for payment of the debt. Once indebted under this system, the life and labor of the tenants and sharecroppers were under the complete direction of the landowners.

The laws supported the employers and the landowners, who also controlled directly or indirectly the administrators of the system of "justice." They defined what was just and what was unjust; they also defined who was just and who was unjust. Naturally (in any dispute) they defined the landowners as the ones who were just and right.

> The manager's job is that of overseeing the work on the plantation and is usually dependent upon his ability to make the plantation pay high profits to the owner, and this frequently depends upon his willingness to exploit the tenants. Under the manager are riding bosses, whose duty it is to superintend or boss a gang of workers on a particular section of the plantation. They usually receive a fixed wage. These men, the riding bosses, are the terror of the plantation. They are the modern equivalent of slave drivers. They are usually uneducated and more often than otherwise are brutal, ruthless and domineering. Nearly all "tote guns" and are often the sheriff's deputies. They maintain with whatever vigor is necessary the iron code of the plantation. They may commit crimes for which the average citizen would be swiftly punished but they are "the law." As an Arkansas sharecropper once aptly observed, "Riding bosses, they ride horses and sharecroppers."[20]

This economic and legal system was thus backed up by white-supported police-state methods. The dissatisfied tenants and share-croppers were threatened, beaten, shot at, burned out of their homes, and finally murdered if they refused to accept and heed the dictates of the white landowners and employers.

The majority of laborers acquiesced out of fear or futility or both, and became near-slaves again. Economically and politically, they were almost as badly situated as slaves. They still lived, for example, in poorly built shacks and on starvation diets.

> On a rickety table they eat their breakfast consisting of biscuits, molasses, and fat-back or, as it is universally known in the South, "sow-belly." Hundreds of thousands of sharecroppers and tenant farmers have never known any other kind of breakfast and today they consider themselves fortunate to have even this. There are thousands, the sharecropper knows, who cry for bread and get none—who make daily trips to the county seat for some groceries and return empty handed, hungry, forlorn,

hopeless. He has seen the children of these disinherited men eat clay. Today they eat clay, tomorrow snakes, the day after tomorrow roots of tender trees.

Another bell rings and the sharecropper and his family trudge toward the cotton patch. Here they work all day, pausing for a while at noon to partake of another meal of cornbread, molasses and meat, or perhaps, as is the case with so many today who cannot afford but two meals a day, just to rest from the terrible ordeal in the fields. When the sun casts its final shadows over the white acres, the family begins the weary walk to the place they call home. Tired, worn, and forlorn they huddle over the table scarcely lit by the kerosene lamp and eat cornbread, molasses and sow-belly. Soon the lamp is turned low. If there is a union meeting or some sort of religious gathering the family may find strength enough left to attend. But most likely the family will "pile" on beds or pallets on the floor, but not to rest, for men's bodies can find no rest on a corn-shuck mattress or on a heap of quilts and rags piled on a pine wood floor.

Of all the dreary sights in the cotton country the most pitiful are the shacks in which the tenants live. Of one, two and three rooms, they are probably the vilest places in which men have to eat and sleep in America.[21]

They were still legally or illegally disfranchised. They still had neither the law nor law enforcers on their side. For many, there was no improvement over slavery in terms of sustenance and comfort. However, in terms of personal liberties and freedom of movement, debt peonage was an improvement over slavery. Proportionately, more blacks could choose their employers; more could choose a wife and raise a family; more were free from being sold or exchanged like a piece of property; more could run away to the North; more could accumulate personal property, however meager; more could move about to talk, to meet, and to exchange ideas; more could engage in collusion with sympathetic whites; more could testify in court; more could bear arms and buy ammunition; more could organize non-violent resistance movements like unions and cooperatives.

In sum, this near-slave status was more advantageous socially and politically than slavery. Debt peonage was harsh and exploitive; yet it afforded blacks more opportunities than did slavery to assault the system. The era of the debt-peonage system was the first time many could assemble, publish, bear arms, marry, move about freely, and organize a strike.

From time to time the sharecroppers and tenant farmers did organize on a multistate basis and call general strikes which forced new prices for cotton. They were able to force concessions from the owners and overseers despite the latter's sociopolitical power and armaments. The Southern Tenant Farmers' Union tried to organize both blacks and whites, and in the process, many organizers were killed. Yet despite the jailings, killings, beatings, kidnappings and the like, the organizers continued.

> There is only one hopeful thing about the situation and that is the Southern Tenant Farmers' Union. Here one may see the truest human values, brotherhood and loyalty and immense courage in the face of danger and here something has happened of terrific historical importance. For the first time in the history of the United States, perhaps in the history of the world, white and colored people are working together in a common cause with complete trust and friendship. They are working together for what is supposed to be everyone's birthright—a decent standard of living, education, security, hope for the future. At present they have none of these things; their only hope of getting them is through their union. The central government has failed them, not through its own fault, but through the deliberate obstruction of the planters and their social system. It is quite clear that the planters want to keep the sharecroppers in a state of slavery. Up to now they have managed to do this.[22]

The material gains, however, were meager and never really changed the economic conditions of the majority, for the buy-on-credit system of the landowners' stores nullified any real financial gains. The more important gain was the sharecroppers' demonstration to themselves that social organization and collective effort could make the owners and merchants listen and take heed even to peons. The movement gave them awareness of their collective power. They discovered a new weapon—collective, nonviolent, direct action. They discovered a new means to force socioeconomic change even when they were impoverished, disfranchised, intimidated, and unrepresented in the judicial, legislative, and executive branches of government.

Blacks during this era became highly politicized. They were involved in several attempts to politically organize the working class whites and blacks into a popular-party movement which was both local and national. Blacks figured importantly in the Populist movement and in the People's Party. The Colored National Farmers Alliance and Cooperative Union was the primary vehicle by which blacks carried on their struggle for social equality and economic betterment.[23] On several occasions they carried out strikes for cotton pickers and other laborers and won. Around the turn of the century, they joined forces with other labor organizations. Laborers' close involvement in the civil-rights movement of the 1960's was a continuation of this early coalition.

Wage Peonage

The wage-peonage system started during the time of slavery, mainly in the cities and towns. In some urban areas, slave owners occasionally hired out their slaves to commercial establishments such as mining companies, factories, and craftshops. The slaves, in effect, were forced to work for wages which were usually collected by their masters. At other times, and under special circumstances, some masters permitted their slaves to find their own employment and hire themselves out.[24] The slaves collected their own wages and turned over the larger portion to their masters. This self-hiring system for wages as slaves rather than as free men and women was one side of the wage-peonage system for Blacks.

By 1850 most of the slaves in cities and towns lived in Mobile, Savannah, Richmond, and Montgomery. Like other urban places, these cities were centers of commerce and government. Urban slaves, like other black laborers, worked in homes, commerce, or factories. Some slaves were independent artisans: A large amount of skilled labor was supplied by black slaves.

In Savannah in 1848, out of a total slave population of 5,686, the larger majority were women and employed as domestics; several hundred men were in manufacturing, commerce, and transportation; 83 were skilled workers.[25]

In such cities in 1840 masters paid from one dollar to three dollars a day for any slave cabinet maker, house or ship carpenter, caulker, bricklayer, blacksmith, tailor, barber, baker, or butcher.[26]

Modern wage peonage thus grew out of the self-hiring of slaves during the last century. Blacks made their entry into manufacturing at this time too, because industrial concerns in the South often owned slaves and preferred slave labor to free wage labor.

Industrial Richmond (Virginia) led in corporate ownership of slaves. Many of them were, of course, unskilled factory hands, but there were a proportion of skilled. More than 54 Richmond corporations owned 100 or more slaves. . . .[27]

In 1850 about 5 percent of the total slave population worked in industry. Most were men and women, but many were children. Of the city- slave population, from 15 to 20 percent were industrial bondsmen, most of whom were owned by the businesses themselves. Hiring slaves directly from other owners was a less popular method, and the least popular was self-hiring by the slaves themselves.[28] Some masters permitted slaves to hire themselves out or, if skilled, to set up their own craftshops. The slaves paid their owners a fixed sum and used the remaining money in any way they wanted. This forced-labor system for wages was another side of the wage-peonage system.

After emancipation, blacks were forced into indebtedness and peonage. The great majority of them remained in the same rural areas of the South where they had been enslaved. In 1880, of all blacks in the United States, 75 percent lived in the former confederate states.[29] In 1890, 57 percent of the Black population were engaged in agriculture, fishing and mining; 31 percent in domestic personal service; and 6 percent in manufacturing. Only 1 percent were engaged in the professions.[30] In 1965, 76 percent of the black workers were still engaged in blue-collar manufacturing, service occupations, and agriculture. Of this total, 55 percent were in service occupations, mostly private household jobs. In that year, blacks were still greatly underrepresented in the following job categories: professional and technical, managerial and proprietorial, clerical, sales, crafts and foremen, farming and farm managing. They were greatly overrepresented in production, nonfarm labor, private household work, services, and as farm laborers and farm foremen.[31] As of 1969, approximately 65 percent of black men and women were still employed as operatives, service workers, private-household workers, nonfarm laborers, farmers, and farm workers.

> In industries with a large proportion of Negro employment, Negroes are much more likely to be lower paid occupations than other employees, except in the local transit and personal services industries. . . .[32]

Also in 1969,

> . . . in the nine industries with relatively high earnings, Negroes had 8% of total employment but only 1% of the higher paid occupations (professional, technical, and managerial).[33]

With all the talk of progress for blacks in occupational achievement, blacks have changed their occupational statuses very little in the one hundred years since emancipation. They still have to work at the lowest-status jobs for the lowest pay. But what should be emphasized is that even in these low-paying jobs they generally fall into the lowest of the low-pay categories. The greatest shift "upward" has been from low-paying agricultural jobs to low-paying service and manufacturing jobs. It should not be surprising that in 1969 the earnings of blacks was still only 61 percent of white earnings.

These data strongly suggest that the wage-peonage system is still with us; only the sectors of employment have changed. Blacks are still predominantly employed in the South, so regional concentration has not changed. The occupational sectors of black employment have changed from rural to urban and from agricultural to manufacturing and commercial. Domestic service is the plight of black women. The conclusion to be drawn is clear: blacks are still rationed the menial low-paying jobs with the least chance of survival in the path of auto-mation, mechanization, and industrial cybernetics.

The job market is still more closed than open to the great majority of black workers. The types of jobs are predetermined by the producer-sellers, as are the wage levels and working conditions. If blacks are going to be consumers in this society, they must work. If they work, they must work at those occupations rationed for blacks, at subsistence wages. The producer-sellers predetermine that millions of blacks will live in poverty whether they work or not.

> About six out of every ten "Negroes and other race" men who were heads of low income families were employed. The comparable figure for men who were heads of white families was five out of every ten.[34]

Surely it can safely be said that more blacks are working at pro-fessional and skilled-level jobs than ever before. But compared to slavery times, the increase is not enough to be called "progress." The great majority of black workers still occupy the same skill levels and pay levels relative to whites as their forefathers did one hundred years ago at the time of emancipation. To be sure, more blacks can hire out their own time now, and they can receive wages which they do not have to share with masters. But considering the various in-equities in the tax structure and the other ways that blacks "pay dues," the forced labor condition of the great majority of black labor-ers is still comparable to that of the urban slaves who used to hire out their own time. Most blacks today receive about 50 to 60 percent of white wages for the same jobs as the urban slaves did at the time of emancipation.

Economic Development and Changing Race Relations

Since 1620, American society has gone through revolutionary economic changes which can be seen in the changing ways Americans
have earned their daily bread and competed in the economic marketplace.

To begin with, ours was an agrarian economy and society; it was an
agricultural society in which small family-owned subsistence farms
dominated the economy even up until 1850. For the most part, these
farms produced few goods for consumption out of the local region
or out of the country even though the plantation system dominated
agricultural export commodities.

Since that time, our society has changed from being primarily
agricultural to being primarily industrial. Industrial commodities of
all types now form the core of local, regional, and national markets, as well as the larger share of our exports. At the same time that
we have been making this qualitative change in the structure of our
economy, we have also been moving from small, noncorporate
enterprises to large, corporate enterprises. Today almost all commodities are produced by these large, corporate industrial concerns; 500
corporations out of more than 200,000 dominate production. This
change has affected the market situation, in that a few large corporations are in a position to monopolize local, regional, and national
markets. Many industries are controlled by monopolies and oligopolies, and such corporations, by their dominance and control, set prices
as well. In oligopolistic and monopolistic markets, prices are determined by the producers-sellers, and the consumers have very little,
if any, opportunity to haggle over prices or to set them in the marketplace. These large, oligopolistic corporations within the various
markets are more interested in how each reacts to the other than in
how consumers react to them, since the individual consumer is, to
some considerable extent, relatively powerless. The large, modern
corporations have, in effect, changed the nature of the marketplaces
for the independent consumers of goods as well as the independent
sellers of labor. The "new industrial state" is out of the control of
common citizens who are bent to the will of the giant corporations.
Even labor has become collectivized, since it has come to be sold
in collective quantities through collective-bargaining processes.[35]

At the same time that the economy has changed in these directions,
the energy sources used in the production of both industrial and
agricultural commodities have changed. Energy produced primarily

by animals or by men has been made obsolete. Most commodities are now produced by machines, which have created an economy requiring very little manpower or animal power. Today whole factories produce thousands of units of goods with only a few men operating the automated-cybernated equipment. Manual laborers no longer have to be dealt with by harsh, direct means such as lockouts, because such workers are increasingly being eliminated. Agricultural jobs have virtually disappeared as occupations, and manual-labor jobs of all types are disappearing at an ever increasing rate.

The jobs which are growing are those termed "skilled technical," as opposed to "unskilled nontechnical." In addition, white-collar jobs—managerial, clerical, and sales—are increasing as blue-collar jobs are decreasing. Blue-collar jobs require workers with qualitatively different training than was required of workers in previous years. Workers with either technical skills or systematic knowledge are now in demand. Workers with either little education, no education, no technical knowledge, or nonscientific knowledge can find few jobs in the economy. In summary, the economy today is largely industrial, mechanized, and dominated by oligopolistic corporations which produce for national and international markets.

Since the economy demands chiefly skilled, white-collar, nonmanual, highly technical personnel, those who cannot qualify because they do not have the requisite skills, knowledge, and performance become the permanently unemployed—the rejects.

These changes have had great economic and social implications for blacks, even though they were not largely or even necessarily racially motivated. In general, nonracial economic motivations have been dominant in most economic changes. But when we were an agrarian society, the southern economy was dependent on the slave labor of blacks only. Black slaves were the chief sources of labor and the chief capital investments. Consequently, slavery by race transformed economic decisions into racial decisions as well. Debt peonage, by contrast, was also a condition of many poor whites so economic decisions during this period became more class-oriented than racial. Debt peonage did not clearly divide white labor from black labor, as did slavery, until economic imperatives forced the end of such an inefficient system of economic distinctions.

As mechanization increased and undermined the agricultural system of the South and as it introduced more efficient means of mass production, it displaced thousands of land-bound blacks. Mechanization also helped to increase the production capacity of industrial corporations of the North, and blacks were attracted to these new urban employment possibilities.

The change from an agrarian to an industrial economy extracted from blacks a heavy price, but it also provided some ways and means for blacks to escape the debt-peonage system. Mechanization and incorporation of industry changed the conditions and loci of racist practices. They also changed the labor markets for millions of citizens, a large number of which were white.

The "new industrial state" of large oligopolistic and monopolistic firms which dominate most of the industries is responsible for the social policy of "integration" and the political policy of "containment." The labor demands are now in the urban factories so blacks have located for the most part in cities to become factory workers in large numbers. The factories require integrated rather than segregated work forces, and white and black workers for the most part are forced to work together. Nevertheless, racial discrimination by job levels and by job pay are economically possible, and so blacks are rationed the lowest-paying, most menial jobs in the new industrial state.

What appears to have happened is that largely economic motives caused the major changes in population distribution and employment opportunities, but within these economic limits, new forms of racial discrimination have been made possible. Economic decisions concerning mechanization, automation, incorporation, conglomeration, and cybernetics were not largely racially motivated decisions, although racially prejudiced men had the opportunities to implement them in racially motivated ways. Even so, these men have had to operate under great economic constraints, and they have allowed more racial equality than they themselves planned on. The white racists have been forced to change their strategies, given the different economic imperatives. Conversely, black protest strategies have changed as the socioeconomic opportunities have changed. They have selected complementary means in each epoch to acquire more and more racial freedom as the economic and demographic conditions have opened up new opportunities.

Economic Versus Political Racism

Some authors[36] have believed that economic forces were the primary causes of the white-over-black racist system. They have maintained that institutionalized racism is the direct result of capitalism. I believe, however, that political motives and racial motives had independent influences in the erection of the white-over-black system. White settlers brought racist and despotic political attitudes with them. They began joining the two sets of ideas before economic exploitation of blacks became a fact. There is evidence that the need for a white Anglo-dominated society was a primary motivation and so I have surmised that the need for perpetual white supremacy caused the white-over-black system to be institutionalized.

The first legislative and judicial acts were racist political acts rather than racist economic acts. Curtailment of political social participation preceded curtailment of economic participation. Separation of the races socially and politically preceded separation of the races economically.

For example, in Virginia, even though the categorical enslavement of Africans did not occur until a statute to that effect was passed in 1670, social separation was already being practiced and enforced by court penalties. In 1630 a white man was ordered by the court to be whipped for violating this social code. In 1688 the court also opined that freedom from bondage did not entitle blacks to all social privileges enjoyed by whites. Further evidence of racial discrimination before full statutory slavery included the police regulations which were passed and denied to blacks alone the right to own guns, poisonous drugs, intoxicants, and white slaves.

There is more historical evidence that antiblack political servility preceded black economic servility. Even blacks of the master estate did not have automatic social equality with white masters and were prohibited by custom and law from exercising the same liberties as whites. It is also abundantly clear that whites enjoyed differential rights through might. Whites had the antiblack attitudes and the legal-political power to back up the attitudes. Blacks were thus initially reduced politically and then economically to a servile state. Economic motives underlay some of the discrimination, but white social and political motives, pure and simple, were even more basic. The "New World" was to be a white Anglo-dominated World.

Racism can operate with any kind of economic system, socialist or capitalist, where discretionary decisions occur with regularity. When economic motives are joined with absolute legal-political power, a variety of socioeconomic arrangements can occur. Racism, as such, operates as a free floating force; it can and does enter into decisions without economic content. And while it can *influence* the emergence, maintenance, and change of economic arrangements, it does not determine the structure of economic systems. Instead, economic systems create the discretionary situations in which racism can operate. Racism colors economic decisions, but legal-political measures make those decisions possible.

I therefore submit that economic means have been only one of several important means used in the attempt to perpetually subjugate blacks. Legal-political measures made possible the economic servility of blacks. Thus, the most basic and primary means in the history of black exploitation in America seem to have been legal-political means since both slavery and debt peonage were instituted and maintained through legal-political power. Even when these economic arrangements became unprofitable, legal-political power alone perpetuated the hierarchical relationship of white over black. The decadent "southern way of life" has been maintained to this day through the power of politics, often with unprofitable results for capitalists.

Political power, as an independent variable, can be made to conform to and protect all types of economically exploitive systems. Without protective·political measures, however, economically exploitive racial arrangements could not be sustained over several generations. Neither economic motives, like profits, nor economic processes, like·competition, are sufficient unto themselves. Likewise racial prejudice alone is not sufficient to institute and perpetuate white-over-black socioeconomic estates. Such institutionalized arrangements have to be implemented and protected through political arrangements· and contrivances—laws, court decisions and police power.

Today the technological possibility exists to eliminate blacks from the work force, since manual labor is increasingly being done by machines. The increasing numbers of permanently unemployed and underemployed in every successive generation of young blacks is evidence of a trend toward elimination. The economic transition from indentured servants to slaves, to peons, to proles, to vagrants is most in evidence for blacks born before 1930, but it should be examined among those born after 1930 as well. This last state of economic obsolescence (vagrancy) suggests a "nuisance" which should be controlled if not eliminated.

Economic devices in and of themselves will not be sufficient to effect social genocide. Political devices like legalized detention centers will have to be used, even though the economic motives may be at the base. Blacks are in a position to be eliminated from the economy today because of past legal-political contrivances which relegated them to the wastelands of the economic system and kept them from competing successfully in the economic marketplaces.

An historical perspective reveals some of the major political decisions which for centuries have determined the economic condition of blacks in America.[37] The first major decision was to make indentured servitude perpetual and lifelong only for blacks. Following that, there were thousands of legal-political decisions to support and maintain that condition. A second major decision came during the founding of this nation in 1775. For some strange reason the Declaration of Independence did not apply to blacks. The founders of this nation had an opportunity to politically abolish the racial oppression the British had forced upon blacks. But what was their answer and rationale? Members of the Constitutional Convention drafted a strong antislavery statement and entered it in the early drafts of the Constitution, but it was finally deleted under pressure from Southerners. At the national Constitutional Convention, the issue of slavery was debated. The northern states for the most part wanted to abolish it, the southern states did not. The Northerners, however, wanted national unity more than the abolition of slavery, and without southern support, the Constitution could not have been ratified. After much debate, slaves were decreed to have both the social and legal qualities of property and of men. This idea became the third politically significant decision when a slave was subsequently declared to be three-fifths of a man. This fractionalization made the issue unequivocally a political fact and not just a philosophical idea. This political compromise constituted the basis for continuing slavery as an economic system. The motivation was mainly economic (especially by the South), and the means were political (especially by the North). A fourth political decision came about fifteen years after the Civil War. This particular decision, described below, constituted the basis for the jim-crow system (the black codes) and accounts for the nonintervention of the federal legislature on the side of blacks for about one hundred years.

The belief was prevalent that the Civil Rights Bill of 1866 could be construed as giving blacks the same rights and privileges as white men with regard to travel, schools, theatres, churches, and the ordinary civil rights which may be legally demanded. A few people even entertained the belief that it also permitted the intermarriage of the races. In addition to this bill, Congress passed and ratified in 1868 the Fourteenth Amendment, declaring that "no State shall make or enforce any law which shall abridge the privileges or immunities of citizens of the United States." Finally, Congress passed the Civil Rights Bill of 1875, entitling blacks to full and equal enjoyment of the accommodations, facilities, and conveyances offered to the public. These bills in addition to the Thirteenth and Fifteenth Amendments made a great impact in the effort to dismantle the white-over-black system.

However, all of this pro-black legislation between 1866 and 1875 was reversed by a court decision in 1883. The Supreme Court, after the "betrayal" of 1877 wherein federal protection of blacks was withdrawn,[38] in effect stated that the Fourteenth Amendment and the other bills refer to actions by the state and not by the individual. The prohibition of individual discrimination was not the subject matter of these federal acts. In short, Congress could pass laws to prohibit acts of discrimination by the state but not by the individual. Thus the federal government could not prevent the establishment of racial discrimination against black Americans as long as that establishment was by individuals and did not have the legal sanction of state statutes. This decision opened the way to racial discrimination by caste rules rather than by legal statutes in permitting individual shopkeepers, innkeepers, and others to deny blacks the rights to public service as matters of individual acts of discrimination. Thus jim crowism, a caste system, was permitted to rise again—to be used to spread and embed racial discrimination in the folkways and mores of the United States, especially in the South. The consequence was that blacks, by caste rules, in mass were denied access to all types of services, goods, jobs, and privileges as well as denied social equality with whites—all under the guise of individual discrimination, which was declared constitutional by the Supreme Court in 1883.

The political racism of the "new industrial state" is more covert and bureaucratic in form and practice, than that of the late 1800's. The laws sanctioning racial discrimination have been taken off the books; the customs have been driven underground. The effects are nevertheless the best evidence of their continued existence. The residential segregation so apparent in neighborhoods, is a political rather than economic outcome. The starvation wage scales in many industries are legal-politically prescribed, not just an outcome of economic market competition. The lack of capital among blacks for investments in businesses is a political contrivance, not the effect of a lack of business interests. Three illustrations will suffice to document the pattern of political racism:

1. For years, housing construction has been federally supported and subsidized. There have been federal regulations guiding the building and financing patterns, as well as the purchasing patterns of this housing. For a long time the Federal Housing Administration (FHA) favored segregated housing and encouraged it. The manual stated: "If a neighborhood is to retain stability, it is necessary that properties shall continue to be occupied by the same society and race group." Under this policy the government refused to subsidize, and therefore discouraged integrated housing. Since a Supreme Court decision in 1948 favoring integrated housing, the practice has been covert. The FHA still supports segregated housing. In fact, many sub-divisions built with FHA support are completely segregated, and the agency contributes to segregation by making it extremely difficult for blacks to "qualify" for such housing. As a result, the FHA loan organization has been primarily a white middle-class housing program. FHA has been and is still guilty of denying blacks subsidized housing in even their restricted housing markets. The white exodus to the suburbs was financed largely by the federal government, at the same time that the containment of blacks in the ghetto was achieved. The housing market is "managed" by politics, not just economic forces.[39]

2. The second example of political racism is found in the sphere of the labor market. One reason that blacks occupy so many low-income jobs is that barriers have been erected to prevent them from getting the better-paying ones. In the skilled trades—one sector of better-paying blue-collar jobs within the easy range of many talented young blacks—the avenues of entry, namely sponsorship and training, are often closed to blacks:

> The Department of Health, Education, and Welfare each year distributes fifty-five millions of dollars of federal funds for education under the Smith-Hughes Act; a very large part of this is given to vocational training programs in which Negroes are totally excluded or limited to unequal, segregated facilities. . . . Thus while white students in vocational schools are preparing for advanced technology in electronics and for the automotive and aero-space industries, Negroes are limited to "home economics" and other traditional service occupations, and here also the federal government has a direct responsibility for helping to perpetuate the pattern that makes the Negro worker and unskilled worker most vulnerable to large-scale permanent unemployment.[40]

The administrators, who are white, straightforwardly practice racial

discrimination. The apprenticeship training, hiring practices, senior-
ity lists, job assignments, and other conditions are regulated by
bureaucratic rules and practices of the unions in those trades, for
example, the building trades. By bureaucratic practices, the unions
have refused for political reasons to admit blacks to the apprenticeship
programs. The National Labor Relations Board and the Department
of Labor have not vigorously enforced the legislative provisions
prohibiting racial discrimination in employment and training programs. It is clear from these effects that Big Government and Big
Labor work hand in hand to prescribe the quantity, the quality, and
the extent of black employment in America. The strongest evidence throughout the years has been the unemployment of those
blacks "qualified" even by the artificially erected standards of both
unions and government. Tests of the marketplace both individually
and collectively in recent years have clearly pointed to the political
racism which has been covertly rampant for years.

3. A third example of how political racism has been used to "contain" blacks is in the area of small-business investment. Until recently,
the federal government virtually refused to grant blacks Small Business Administration (SBA) loans.[41] Very few blacks could "qualify"
for such loans. In short, the federal government itself raised high barriers to entry and acted along with white insurance companies to
effectively block black investments in the business world. More
recently, the SBA changed its political practices and found that loans
to blacks can be good, sound investments, having learned that loans
made to Blacks who were previously considered high risks have a
relatively low default rate. The SBA has accelerated its aid to black
businessmen, a fact which demonstrates that it was a political rather
than an economic matter which governed and still is governing the
flow of investment money to blacks. Because of years and years of
political racism in government-subsidy programs, the present governmental actions to help blacks overcome one of the major barriers to
entry into business enterprises are too little, too late, and in the wrong
types of investments.

The polity has been most instrumental in subjugating blacks. It has
"managed" the economy in ways to restrict economic forces from·
operating freely. In a free and open system, many blacks would succeed. To avert such success, the politicos and administrators pursue
political policies and practices to keep blacks relatively economically
disadvantaged.

3 Estate, Caste, and Class

Almost from its beginning, the U.S. power elite attempted to construct one set of rights and privileges for blacks and a separate and different set for whites. As a result, blacks in America have suffered under several different forms of restrictions and exploitation. The most rigid and lasting form of exploitation and deprivation has been the white-over-black estate system. An estate system, as we have already discussed, is a hierarchy of groups defined by law in which the rights, privileges, and duties of each group are specified by laws.

In America after 1660, the Africans who came to the New World became subjected to estate requirements and restrictions. Within a period of a few decades, many Africans who had arrived after 1619 were deprived of the legal rights and privileges which were enjoyed by their white counterparts. The newly arriving blacks were forced into a state of perpetual servitude by laws to that effect. Blacks were restricted to the servant status without opportunity to end the indenture. Subsequent laws eventually permitted the denial of all legal rights and privileges enjoyed by white citizens.

A second set of conditions which have been forced on blacks are caste conditions. A caste system is a hierarchy of social groups whose rights, privileges, and duties are defined by social codes and enforced mainly by private, but sometimes by public, means. Like estates, the caste groups are virtually endogamous and hereditary. In the U.S., the social codes were racist antiblack prescriptions and proscriptions, sometimes referred to as "racial etiquette," which governed the demeanor and deference of blacks as well as their aspirations and achievements vis-a-vis, of course, the whites. Antiblack codes started in practice before statutory slavery and no doubt encouraged the racist legislators who dreamed up the statutory white-over-black estate system. Antiblack codes over the years have been rigid, extensive, and lasting, and they have governed the everyday extra-legal relations of blacks and whites at the most elementary levels and in the most intimate areas of human association. This elaborate social system of racial practices is a caste system of social relations.

Finally, blacks have suffered under a set of class conditions. A class system is a hierarchy of income and occupational groups which enjoy similar marketplace life-chances; that is, they have attained similar monetary and proprietary achievements. Their rights, privileges, and duties arise from economic circumstances. Blacks have been underachievers in monetary and proprietary contests, but this has been largely the result of the restricted market practices of whites who have consistently denied blacks equal opportunities for gainful employment and for acquisition of property.

While European immigrants mainly suffered class discrimination alone, blacks have suffered estate, caste, and class discrimination as well. The dynamics of class and caste struggles are different from the dynamics of estate struggles. Estates are established by law, and in fact, they can only be changed by law. They force the black struggle to be concerned with litigation and legislation as primary tactics for changing institutional racism. Blacks have successfully resisted and attacked the estate conditions by using these tactics as well as propagandization to change the legal circumstances which have given whites the right to exploit blacks while excluding them from full enjoyment of the rights and privileges whites enjoy.

Blacks have had to be concerned with attacking the caste conditions as well. They have used various forms of nonviolent direct action, in the form of demonstrations, strikes, pickets, boycotts, sit-ins, kneel-ins, and pray-ins. They came finally to insubordination in the form of direct physical resistance to whites who persisted in attempting to force blacks to accept a low ascribed status. Caste conditions have been more visible, more widely practiced, and more popularly white-supported than either estate or class conditions. Social codes were more extensive than estate laws, and all over the United States the caste conditions became socially accepted in the behavior of both

laymen and law enforcement officials. Even after slavery was statu-
torily eliminated, caste discrimination continued, and, in fact, it
would be very difficult even today to find any white person who has
not acted in caste ways. Castes have been a permanent part of life in
the U.S.

In addition to racially discriminatory estate and caste codes, blacks
have suffered economic discrimination. What I mean is that there have
been budgetary and employment decisions which have resulted in the
restriction of full black participation in the economy of the American
society. These racist economic decisions were used to deny blacks equity
in occupations and remunerations. For example even today black and
white baseball players of similar ability do not get the same pay:
Whites get more than their black counterparts. This economic racism
gives us a glimpse of how racial discrimination in salaries and wages
occurs among those individuals of similar abilities. Moreover, racist
employers can maintain the white-over-black class system even in
situations where whites perform in inferior ways to blacks. This set of
economic practices has a long history in American society and is one
of the reasons why black college graduates make about the same amount
of money on the average as white high school graduates.

Recognizing that they suffer economic and class discrimination,
blacks have countered with class actions. They have tried educational
improvement, occupational improvement, and skills improvement
in attempts to minimize the bases for the class discrimination which
is so acceptable and so extensively practiced in the United States. Mis-
takenly, blacks have thought that individual self-improvement
would be sufficient to overcome caste and estate conditions too, but
the black bourgeoisie proved to themselves and to other blacks that
high occupational and educational achievements in themselves do not
eliminate the antiblack social codes and the antiblacks laws. The
removal of antiblack laws and the antiblack codes, they learned,
requires a different set of strategies than individual self-improvement;
hence they have embarked on political movements in order to bring
down the American institutional racist establishments.

Blacks have had to engage in a three-pronged attack on the racist
institutions of the United States. They have had to be social, political,
economic, and legal thinkers in order to figure out how to overcome
the degradation and exploitation which was being perpetrated upon
them by the racist systems of white-over-black estate, castes, and class
conditions. They have had to sort out the forces of deprivation and
exploitation, and come up with counter forces to overcome this situation. In the process, blacks have espoused such ultimate goals as

emigration, secession, separation, integration, and revolution, and have established various organizations to work on achieving them. The Universal Negro Improvement Association established by Marcus Garvey worked toward emigration; The Republic of New Africa is a secessionist endeavor; The Congress of Racial Equality strives for separatism; while the National Association for the Advancement of Colored People as well as the National Urban League and the Southern Christian Leadership Conference have all been integrationist endeavors; and finally, the Black Panther Party and the Congress of African Peoples have been revolutionist struggles. These examples make it clear that blacks have not been single-minded in their approach to liberation. They have been using a variety of means by which to extricate themselves from the shackles of racism. The situation has been difficult for blacks in the United States because the estate, caste, and class conditions have been so highly interlocking and interpenetrating. The laws, for example, often restricted blacks to the practice of certain classes of labor and to the learning of certain classes of skills, knowledge, and performance. Such restrictions predetermined the underachievement of monetary and proprietary gains, for they determined that blacks would be unable to acquire the wherewithal to finance their own self-help projects even where they had the motivation to do so. By law, blacks were forced to be subordinate in class to their white counterparts and even to their white inferiors. In addition to the laws, the racists were able to put into operation antiblack codes, both inside and outside the law, which denied blacks full social, political, and employment opportunities, encouraged white employers to deny opportunitues to qualified blacks, and permitted them to pay blacks less than the going rates for the types of performances they were capable of giving. Similar antiblack codes encouraged politicians to act prejudicially in judgments of literacy tests, understanding tests, and other qualifying tests. Under such circumstances, whites could not help defining themselves and their skin color as superior and somehow intrinsically of more worth than black skin color. It is clear that the interpenetration of the laws with the social codes and of the codes with market discrimination made blacks realize a need for a multifaceted approach to liberation. Racist laws, codes, and market decisions have maintained an elaborate white-over-black system for three hundred years, and the interlocking relationship of estate, caste, and class explains why blacks have had difficulty overcoming racism in the United States.

As one observes the behavior of white clerks, employers, politicians, bureaucrats, and laymen, it is hard to tell whether they are being driven by estate, caste, or class forces. Estate, caste, and class prescriptions and proscriptions probably enter into all institutionalized racism. Whenever antiblack laws have been eliminated, discriminatory caste codes have filled the voids and whites have thereby perpetuated the white-over-black system long after the laws have been taken off the books. Witness efforts toward school desegregation, equal employment, open housing, and voter registration. These efforts have been nullified by caste and class forms of discrimination which have been used in one way or another to continue to deny blacks their rightful opportunities even when there has been legislation to eliminate legal bases for discrimination. Racial change, therefore, has been slow and many strategies other than litigation and legislation have been needed to turn the tide of institutionalized racism in the United States. Whites have spent more than two hundred years structuring racist barriers and traps of many different forms. To overcome them, blacks have had to develop a multiple offense and had to open up many warfronts. Blacks have had to use every conceivable humane means for changing the system and they have had to remain flexible in order to counter the many complex institutional actions which have denied them their just rights and privileges in American society.

Stratification in the U. S. has been manifold, and various cultural, racial, and sexual groups have suffered under it. Racial and sexual minorities have most often been subjected to estate discrimination; racial, immigrant, and sexual minorities have all been subjected to caste discrimination; virtually every type of group has suffered from class discrimination. These are different type conditions, and hence they help to explain some of the differential successes various groups have had achieving money, property, and power in American society. Many European immigrants who came to America suffered caste and class discrimination, but they did not labor under a multitude of estate restrictions. They have not been subjected to official genocide, chattel slavery, human degradation and cultural mortification. Those caste rules which did exist to govern the relationships between European immigrants and other Americans were not so highly institutionalized and enforced as the laws governing the racial minorities. On the other hand caste rules regulating racial minorities in the United States have been so widely supported by white people that only the federal government could effectively challenge the enforcement of such rules at the state and local levels.

The civil rights movement of the 1960's testifies to the tenacity with which caste rules have been practiced and enforced. This movement is also documentary proof of how differently Africans and Europeans were treated in America. The scope and depth of discrimination against blacks was far worse than the discrimination against Europeans. Hence, it does not make sense to ask why blacks have not advanced so rapidly as have Europeans. Europeans have always been favored over blacks and have not been restricted in the same ways. A look at the comparative legal and sociocultural histories of the two groups raises in sharp relief the fact that Europeans coming to the U.S. were given boots and bootstraps by which to pull themselves up, while for blacks this was not so. It is clear that the European immigrants in America have been moving largely from a caste discrimination and mild caste status at that, to a class discrimination. But Africans in America have been moving from caste and estate discrimination to class discrimination. Estate and caste have been more rigid and exploitive over these past three hundred years than class has been. Class discrimination, exclusive of estate and caste restrictions, is more changeable. In a class system blacks have more chances to achieve rewards from their labors; they would have more advancement in monetary and proprietary matters. Once racial discrimination is eliminated, class discrimination will remain another problem to be solved.

Three Hundred Years of Estate, Caste and Class Conflicts

Since 1660, the history of blacks in the U.S. has been a history of a people's valiant struggle for human rights. By overt and covert methods blacks have fought white racists throughout these three hundred years. They have fought even as the obvious advantage in the conflict has been on the side of whites controlling as they did a virtual monopoly of all tangible and intangible means of coercion and violence in the society to establish and maintain several interlocking systems of economic and social exploitation. The first establishment was the forced-labor system of *chattel slavery*, which reduced most blacks to a state of perpetual, involuntary servitude. But before slavery was established, whites began using laws to disfranchise blacks, and within a few decades, blacks were fully disfranchised, economically dispossessed, educationally stymied, and socially degraded. Racist demagogues through white despotism devised social, economic, and political statutes to reduce blacks to servility. This political and economic bondage facilitated the use of every conceivable coercive means possible to turn once-proud African warriors into cringing, submissive, childlike beasts of burden. But they failed, and legal-political despotism eventually had to be extended to virtually every member of the white estate, wherein antislavery whites had to be coerced into supporting the laws and practices to perpetuate black servility. Legal and moral prohibitions against white atrocities were removed by racist laws which protected and gave moral support to the whites who practiced racist oppression. White judges, eventually decreed that black slaves had no legal or human rights that whites needed to respect. This cleared the way for whites to constantly beat, maim and even kill blacks when they resisted oppression and exploitation in any way. For example, if a black raised his hand in self defense, he could justifiably be killed. In sum, whites strove hard to "mortify" blacks culturally, socially and psychologically by stripping them of property rights, political privileges, economic opportunities and human rights.

Through a system of white despotism and chattel slavery the racists succeeded in extracting labor free from millions of blacks for more than two hundred years.

Outnumbered, overpowered, and against overwhelming odds, blacks resisted. During the two hundred years of slavery through determination, intellectual and social astuteness they invented various physical, economic, and social means of overthrowing the slavocracy. They used legislative, litigatory, and propagandistic tactics to chip away at the slavocracy. Struggling day by day with only the most meager means against a violent, despotic enemy, blacks asked for and received the help of Indians and white sympathizers. These coalitional efforts also proved to be instrumental in the bringing down the slavocracy. Using all means possible, blacks chipped away at its foundation slowly and methodically, for they and their allies could not abolish it in one mighty blow.

Blacks counterattacked *white despotism* and *chattel slavery* with both violent and nonviolent *black abolitionism*. Slave revolts, individual or collective, are evidence of this abolitionist movement. Court decisions and civil rights laws represent the successes of this movement. Abolition activities were quite naturally "illegal" for slaves and included such activities as the destruction of white life and property, the disruption of the economic production processes, emigration by stealth (flight), and in some cases even manumission. Blacks who were not slaves had some other ways of fighting to eliminate slavery. With access to printing equipment, some engaged in political propagandizing. With access to white lawyers and legislators, others used litigatory and legislative means. With access to financial means, still others emigrated to Africa or the Caribbean. Finally, there were those blacks who sought to be assimilated, to compete as laborers and consumers in the economic marketplace, to prove to whites they were mistaken about black intelligence and skill. Through "integration" and the acquisition of wealth, they could purchase the freedom of friends and relatives still in slavery.

Once the Emancipation Proclamation took effect blacks became committed to the programs of *black assimilationism* which seemed to be oriented towards the political, economic, and educational integration and betterment of black citizens. They began making improvement through welfare legislation and economic competition and by these means, were able to begin overcoming some of the marks of servility.

Within the brief span of a decade this is in fact what happened, as thousands of blacks assimilated politically, educationally, and economically. But emancipation was not to be. Predictably, the white supremacists recuperated from the ravages of the Civil War, and violently rose up to stop black assimilationism. Whites intimidated, assaulted and killed blacks who dared try to better themselves. Whites eventually erected a second barrier of anti-black codes resulting in further social, economic, and political oppression and exploitation. Rural chattel slavery was transformed into a *debt-peonage, share-cropping, tenant-farming system*; and urban chattel slavery was transformed into a *wage-peonage factory system*, which relegated marginal, unstable, low-paying industrial and service jobs to blacks.

This new anti-black establishment joined political jim crowism with economic *debt peonage* and *wage peonage*, using black codes and terror tactics to reintroduce black political disfranchisement, segregation and social degradation. With this system, whites effectively slowed down black assimilationism; they effectively prevented the blacks from enjoying their share of political power as well as economic and educational betterment. With the machinations of jim crowism, whites concocted the numerous sociopolitical disadvantages: "segregation" they called it. Segregation became in fact the social system of race etiquette which they had begun in cities during the period of chattel slavery to govern all primary and secondary relations between blacks and whites. Before the Civil War whites erected a man-brute establishment; now it was to be a man-boy establishment. Naturally, blacks rebelled as they had always done, but whites were equally persistent. Using various legal and nonlegal devices, whites forced their system of race etiquette on blacks. Whites forced blacks to esteem, respect, and honor them, and forcibly prescribed for blacks how to act, what work to do, and what to aspire for in life. By mob terrorism, judicial punishment and police tyranny, they coerced blacks into overt acquiescence. When blacks attempted to vote, run for public offices, file petitions in courts, and petition legislatures for redress of their grievances, whites, who controlled all of these institutions, suppressed these activities by all means at their disposal. Racial justice was out of the question. White supremacy was the name of the game. Blacks, however, launched still another counter-attack to overcome this combination of debt and wage peonage and jim crowism. Many took refuge in the North; a few, however, fled to Liberia, in Africa, and still others to Canada. Nevertheless, some blacks assimilated economically, politically, educationally, and socially, thus beginning a second phase of black abolitionism and assimilationism. I call this phase *black neo-abolitionism* and *neo-assimilationism.*

For more than fifty years, blacks counterattacked the jim crow establishment with litigation, legislation, migration and non-violent direct action with the consequence of forcing the economic system of rural debt peonage to give way almost entirely to wage peonage. Numerous black sharecroppers and tenant-farmers, for example, around the turn of this century helped force the introduction of mechanization and industrialization into the South by work slowdowns, strikes, and other disruptive behavior. Blacks helped to make the rural debt-peonage system of production more costly than mechanized production. In contrast with mechanization, peonage was made increasingly more inefficient as a means of holding laborers. Indebtedness became a more inefficient system of motivating the black laborers to work. Although debt peonage could never bring out the best efforts of black laborers, that system of production and management became very wasteful in comparison to other available means: machines and cheap or free labor. When this point of diminishing returns was reached, whites stopped forcing blacks to stay on the plantations, and white employers stopped blocking the train stations and highways to keep blacks from leaving the South.

Gradually but methodically, in protest, millions of blacks left the farms and migrated to the southern and northern cities. They sought jobs in manufacturing where the relatively better opportunities for advancement were. They found, however, another system of economic peonage long operating there too—*wage peonage*. But, it was better than indebtedness. *Wage peonage* had a long history: Long before the Emacipation Proclamation, urban whites had restricted most blacks to the marginal, low-paying jobs that white laborers themselves did not want. These menial subservient jobs, in effect, forced most blacks to continue to be a subordinate class to their white counterparts. White employers rationed those jobs which afforded blacks only a marginal economic existence—jobs which were high-risks, unstable, temporary, or seasonal in nature. These jobs condemned most urban blacks to perennial poverty even if they worked fulltime. Private and public corporations were not exceptions; they practiced *stratified integration* with educated blacks: that is, they restricted even educated blacks also to 'marginal, low paying jobs. Wage peonage was the economic practice of the day and *stratified integration* was the political mechanism.

Despite the hardship of wage peonage, thousands of rural blacks fled sharecropping and tenant-farming to become wage laborers in factories and in various private and public corporate enterprises. As meager as these gains were, they appeared to be better than the rural *debt-peonage* system which was the only other alternative. *Stratified integration* was better than no integration at all, better than segregation. Wage peonage became one of the prices blacks had to pay to participate in the industrial system of the cities. Stratified integration became the entrance price into the factory system. Horizontal integration without vertical integration was the norm.

As we have intimated, whites combined *wage peonage* with *token integrationism*. Whites were willing to integrate minimally as long as they retained their superordinate positions of power and privileges. *Stratified integrationism* eschewing strict segregationism made possible the present day *wage-peonage system*.

Blacks grew tired of being on the bottom after a while and refused to be contented and satisfied. They counterattacked this system too and moved aggressively to break up the system of *stratified integration* by forcing owners to hire qualified blacks not merely for the low-level jobs but also for the middle-level positions in both public and private corporations. Once again blacks accelerated the abolition and assimilation attack by picketing, marching, boycotting, and using all types of disruptive civil disobedience. The main character of the black movement this time was nonviolent. After continuous black agitation, demonstration and disruption, many white leaders in public and private corporations reluctantly conceded and rationed more middle-level positions to blacks. Vertical integration became the goal of blacks in earnest now.

Integration remained token. It became a type of co-optation in which the white institutions "let in" a certain number of blacks in order to appease the militants and then control, and neutralize the aspiring blacks from within. By this device, the whites, in effect, took the initiative and control of the black assimilationism: they determined its quality, rate, and extent of assimilation-integration. Black assimilation became more rhetoric than real, because whites still controlled the terms of integration. Socioeconomic betterment through social assimilation-integration turned out to be a pipedream for most blacks—even for the black Bourgeoisie.

Recent integration has nevertheless left blacks white-dominated, white-controlled, and white-directed. It has made them "whitewardly" oriented. But frustration with this white-ward movement is causing groups of blacks to violently revolt against integrationism, both ideologically and organizationally. The new black revolt is causing blacks to put whites out of their minds and out of their black organizations. It is leading to a renaissance of Africanism in all forms: language, clothes, food, social structure, and so on. It is leading to separatism.

In this new movement and epoch, blacks are wanting to separate communally and nationally. Some blacks want communal social separation, African reacculturation, and black economic self-help. Others want complete national separation from the U.S. *Black separatism* is the fastest-growing black political-economic doctrine of the day among blacks, but it has come programmatically to mean communal betterment—a type of macro-integration.

Faced with the gradualism, obstructionism, and nullification of the present-day white integrationist, the black separatists have called upon the reluctant black masses to seek their own black base of power. Black separation advocates insist that blacks control their own work places, schools, and marketplaces and thereby provide for their own security; CORE and other civil-rights organizations have mobilized fully around these new programs of communal separation—the way to black betterment.

White supremacists, as always, have started their moves to neutralize and nullify these separatists. The counter political doctrine of whites seems to be *containmentism*: whites have embarked on a movement to segregate blacks in the decaying ghettos as long as possible. The political doctrine of *containmentism* builds upon and reinforces the com munal separatism of blacks and would limit blacks to better conditions only *within* the ghettos but not to bridge the social and economic distance *between* the black ghettos and the white suburbs. It calls for discouraging and resisting open housing and busing children to and from the ghettos. It also calls for relocating businesses to the suburbs.

Economic, educational, and political containment is the white racist trend of the day. Accordingly, the new economic trap for blacks is coming to be public employment and public assistance, the beginnings of *welfare peonage* which fit functionally with the eroding, decaying inner cities where blacks are to be confined. If communal separatists want to "control" that economically decaying territory, white racist leaders will let them do it. Blacks, however, must not disrupt the white corporate industrial, retail, and financial processes; they must not insist on living in the white neighborhoods before whites are ready to give them up; and they must not press for busing children across districts to achieve racial balance in schools. Hence, black communalism and black culturalism, like black capitalism, have been targeted for being co-opted and controlled by *white containmentism*, which is the newest emerging political form of the white-over-black system. If this situation suggests a bad time for blacks, the politics of racial stratifications outlined in this book suggests the conclusion that blacks will overcome this latest oppression (*containmentism*) through the same probe-assault-change processes they have been using for the past three hundred years. The history of black-white conflict leads me to conclude that since blacks have been breaking down the estate-caste-class establishment and its attendant entrapments and since blacks have been attaining more and more legal, social, and territorial liberation, this latest repression attempt by whites will not succeed despite predictions of impending black genocide. If we remember that once blacks have made gains, they have never been forced to relinquish all gains and revert to their original position—even in the face of violent white repression—then predictably the newest white containment establishment will therefore be met with more probes and assaults followed by changes towards liberation. The nature of the black liberation movements today would seem to suggest the black attack on ghetto containment will come through mass national separation movements or revolutionary movements.

National political, economic, and social separation will become more attractive to blacks only after the failure of communal separation. National independence in the modern world is certainly only a matter of degrees, but the degrees of freedom for blacks with national independence will be quite an advancement after *containmentism* joined with *welfare peonage* is experienced to the fullest.

4 Black Liberation Strategies

There have been seven basic black liberation strategies used unevenly over the past three hundred years due to a combination of social, economic, judicial and legislative obstacles employed by the dominant group. At the present time, these strategies are still being employed as conditions warrant.

The liberation strategies are destruction, nonviolent direct action, emigration, education, economic betterment, legislation, and litigation. Judging by the outcomes of these efforts, it is clear that blacks have been trying to overthrow institutionalized despotism and racism—the greatest obstacles to black economic and social betterment. Contrary to popular notions about blacks being just another immigrant group trying to raise themselves economically, the historical record shows that blacks have not been reluctant to engage in economic competition as much as they have been denied by law the opportunities to compete successfully. In short, they have had much more than a class problem; they have had at base an estate problem supported by a caste problem, which have been imposed by whites themselves. All the economic betterment in the world does not eliminate estate and caste limitations. Class can exist within caste and estate limitations. For example, a person may enjoy his life better as a rich member of a subordinate legal estate or caste, but so long as he is estate-bound and caste-bound, he is not an equal citizen of the nation in which he lives.

He is always under the domination and control of the superordinate group. In a word, separate development within apartheid is still subordination of blacks and superordination of whites.

The ways blacks have sought to overthrow the estate and caste domination by whites are presented below, within the four periods of black assault: abolitionism, assimilationism, neo-abolitionism and neo-assimilationism and separatism.

Destruction

Blacks revolted violently from the time they were snatched from African shores. Many were so incorrigible that official bulletins labeled some tribes as "rebellious." Slaves were reported to have revolted during Columbus' second voyage. Before 1619, the year blacks were first brought to the American colonies, Blacks had already revolted in Hispaniola, Puerto Rico, Panama, Cuba, and Mexico.[1]

The tradition of violent slave rebellions in the U.S. goes back to the period of white and black indentured servitude. Biracial rebellions of servants, both white and black were common. As blacks became the only perpetual servants, the servant revolts became uniquely black revolts. Blacks rebelled in many ways by individual and collective acts of rebellion such as verbal and physical attacks on overseers and masters. It was also common for slaves to fight back when beaten. Frederick Douglass, one such rebellious slave, (reportedly) concluded that "he who is whipped easiest is whipped most often." It was costly for some slaves to rebel, but many did.

The individual acts of destruction were quite varied, and included the use of arson, the maiming of animals, and the breaking of tools. This type of sabotage was used regularly and systematically to disrupt production. Broken plows, harnesses, hoes, and other equipment and also maimed mules, horses, and oxen helped to crush the slavocracy.

> Slaves seem to have taken the greatest delight in abusing the horses, oxen and mules that were so essential to the day to day work of the plantations . . . there was no substitute for work animals.[2]

Work animals were critical factors in the economic success of the slave states, and the slaves focused on this critical element of production. Through their concerted efforts, they forced whites to discontinue using the more efficient but less durable horses and forced them to use the less efficient but more durable oxen and mules.

. . . the larger the slave force the greater the dependence upon mules
and oxen relative to the faster, more efficient horses, presumably because
horses cannot take as much abuse as mules and need more care and more
skill in driving.[3]

Work animals required at least a minimal amount of maintenance
and care, but the slaves, in large number, simply refused to provide
this service. Consequently, this neglect contributed to the higher cost
of slave-produced products. To be sure, many factors caused the agrarian slave labor to compete poorly with the industrial free-labor economy, but the one important cause of the slower growth and lower efficiency of the agrarian system was the resistance and sabotage of rebellious slaves.

As collective action, rebellions took some different forms. One quite
common form of collective rebellion was guerrilla warfare. Rebellious
slaves often ran off together to live in the woods and the swamps, and
from this vantage point, they raided the plantations and homes of the
white masters, killing, burning, looting, and destroying everything
in sight. Evidence of these occurrences can be found in U.S. Army
campaign records.and in the newspaper files of Southern papers like
the *Norfolk Herald* and the *Richmond Examiner*.

Direct insurrections by five or more slaves were less common than
guerrilla activities, but still numerous. There were more than four
hundred plots and conspiracies, or actual insurrections, discovered
and recorded during the period of slavery. Black slaves, through these
insurrections, sought to overthrow the white leaders who were oppressing them, because for most slaves, white controlled plantation life was
the only societal system they knew; the plantation was the limit of
their world view and life-space. Like true revolutionaries, they fought
to control that life-space and they did it in the direct and classical way.
They seized whatever means of violence they could find and they tried
to overthrow the owners of the means of production and administration. Violent abolitionism was always on the conscience of whites,
who lived in constant fear of any overt or covert signs of such movements. Four notable periods have been identified as times of an unusual
number of slave revolts: 1710-1721, 1790-1802, 1821-1832, and 1850-
1860. Not unlike the latest contemporary ghetto uprising which also
came in a wave between 1964-1968, the slaves of that day also retaliated
against the relative deterioration in their economic and political
conditions.

The second period, that of black assimilationism, was quit
in that blacks went about the business of personal and ...aterial
betterment. They worked hard, bought property, engaged in politics,
and began educating their children. Such a radical shift in the status
and privileges of blacks was exasperating to whites. The "white way
of life" was fading away. The social and psychological conditions of
survival and well-being were being supplanted with some new
conditions which were unfamiliar and threatening. Predictably,
whites resisted, since legally and politically they had lost control
in several states. So they took to the streets and roads, murdering,
maiming, and whipping blacks into acquiescence. The white lynch
mob became commonplace throughout the country. The Reconstruction Period was one of the most brutal and bloody in all of American
history. Whites in both the North and the South lynched or massacred
Blacks by the thousands. This assault against blacks started right
after the Civil War and continued through the turn of the century,
having reached a peak during the 1890's.

The strategy of destruction was not widely used by blacks during this
period. Destruction by blacks took the form of uprisings and mutinies.

> The Elaine (Arkansas) uprising and the several mutinies which occurred
> during the War make up the bulk of cases of direct assaults by Negroes
> upon the accommodative structure.[4]

During each riot or pogrom, scores of blacks were murdered and just
a few whites were reported killed. Blacks were limited to self-defensive violence inasmuch as the means of the burning, looting, killing,
whipping, maiming, intimidating, and persecuting were confined
primarily as in the past to the members of the white estate.

Blacks did not start really fighting back, using black violence
against white violence, until 1919.[5] The period from 1919 to 1965
has been a time of neo-abolitionism and neo-assimilationism where
the NAACP and the National Urban League have been the most
prominent forces of assimilation and abolition, but there has been
retaliatory violence used by blacks without their support.

The race riots which took place during this time differed from those
of the past. Formerly, blacks rarely fought back, so that few whites
in comparison to blacks were killed. But during the Washington, D.C.,
riot of 1919, Blacks did fight back and the casualties were more nearly
equal on each side. During the Chicago riot of 1919, the same pattern

obtained. Twenty-three whites and fifteen blacks were killed, indicating again the willingness of blacks to fight back. From 1919 to 1960, several riots occured, and in all of them blacks fought back. Detroit and New York had race riots in 1943, and the retaliatory pattern continued. For example, in Detroit, besides those blacks killed by police, there were eight whites and nine blacks killed. The police killed seventeen blacks and no whites. In the Harlem riot of 1943, the retaliation was mostly against white-owned property and white policemen.

What this historical review indicates is that the strategy of destruction was not extensively used by blacks during the first assimilation period. However, the second assimilation period, retaliatory rioting was more frequent but it still was not the main strategy for blacks in their drive for assimilation into the whole society of the United States. It was not until the middle 1960's that rioting came to be a tactical assault weapon, consciously used to win certain concessions from whites. Before this time, rioting was used only in self-defense or in immediate retaliation for a white assault upon members of the black communities.

Three hundred years after the first slave uprisings, blacks have returned to using violent, collective, direct action against the properties of whites. The new wave of assaults began in 1965 in Watts, a section of Los Angeles, California.[6] Touched off by a police incident, blacks began burning apartment buildings, stores, offices, and factories. They looted the stores and, with sniper fire, kept firemen from putting out the fires. Two years later, in 1967, an even larger rebellion of the same kind took place in Detroit. The same behaviors as in Watts were repeated but on a larger scale. The Detroit rebellion ignited rebellions by blacks in more than thirty cities large and small. While the precipitating factor was a police incident, the underlying cause was the persistent racism which had left a large number of blacks either underemployed or unemployed. In addition, the racism perpetrated by the administrators of "law and order" became so flagrant that blacks felt compelled to use retaliatory action. Since that time during nearly every summer since 1965, rioting, looting, and shooting have broken out in American cities. During 1967, a high point for the recent black revolts, about 160 notable riots or "civil disorders" were recorded by officials of the national government. These riots occurred in 128 different cities of all sizes. Damaged property or losses due to looting or other confiscatory activities has been estimated to be over $100,000,000 with around $50,000,000 worth of damage and losses occurring in Detroit alone.

Currently violent blacks are beginning to organize again for self-defense and for offense against racists and racist institutions. These black organizations presently have only small numbers, meager financial means and material armaments, but despite these deficiences, the evidence indicates that new levels of dedication and readiness are being established. Paramilitary organizations like the Black Panthers have already begun to form and there have been some confrontations with police units in some of the larger cities.[7] The next epoch will see an escalation of paramilitary operations by blacks in their attempts to use whatever assault strategies are necessary to change the racist system. Because whites have historically used whatever means *necessary* to maintain their racism, blacks have been forced to develop all means *possible* to use against the institutionalized racism which continues to subjugate, exploit, and annihilate them in so many overt and covert ways. Black separatism is the latest rally cry.

Suprisingly, however, white Americans do respond constructively at times to black demonstrations of unrest and resentment. In Detroit for example business and civic leaders formed a committee to correct some of the inequities of the system. They began neighborhood improvement programs, job training programs, job upgrading programs, renewal programs and black business programs. These official responses added credibility to the blacks' claims about the inequalities in the distribution of jobs and other means for sustenance and comfort. Accordingly, a national group of business and civil rights leaders was formed called the Urban Coalition. The Coalition set for itself the task of finding or creating 1,000,000 jobs for black Americans. On the heels of this coalition came 350 insurance companies who set out to formulate a program to invest $1,000,000,000 in slum redevelopment. To be sure, these are only beginnings which will require time to come to fruition. Nevertheless, these beginnings are significant because they represent some political gain from violent revolts.

Nonviolent Direct Action

Black people in America have been struggling for complete liberation for more than three hundred years. They have used a variety of strategies in order to liberate themselves, and nonviolent direct action has constituted a major technique in this struggle for liberation. At first glance, it might not appear that the struggle has been continuous, but upon close examination it becomes evident that the effort has been uninterrupted. Nonviolent direct action strategies in the early days of black abolitionism took the form of work slowdowns, strikes, work boycotts, and individual disobedience. For moral and material reasons, many slaves did not believe in the possibility of violently overthrowing the system. Therefore, they substituted other means to bring down the racist institution. The slaves resisted their white subjugators in many forms in hundreds of instances, but the form most commonly used was that of nonviolent direct action. The results of this kind of resistance—namely, the attack on the process of production—were notable and recognized by many. Historians have written about the high cost of slavery as a mode of production, especially in comparison to a system of free laborers and of wage-price competition. Strikes, slowdowns, boycotts, and individual disobedience, substantially restricted output and the result was increased production cost. By these means, slaves helped to increase the prices of the final products. The material consequence was to inflate the prices of slave labor products in comparison to the value of the products of free labor. In addition, slave resistance diminished both the quality of many products and the efficiency of the production process, thereby forcing the owners to use more supervisors than would have been needed in a system of free laborers, who were highly motivated to work. The cost of supervision became an important additional production expense, and in time, costs of slave labor became prohibitive for some slave owners.

While many slaves worked diligently, many more tried to make slavery economically very costly. They used every nonviolent means they discovered.

> They could be made to work reasonably well under close supervision in the cotton fields, but the cost of supervising them in more than one or two operations at a time was prohibitive.[8]

When they made supervision more costly, they were undermining the system of slavery. When they were not being self-directive, they made the cost of motivating them another expense. For many owners, therefore the difference in cost between maintaining unmotivated, unpaid slaves and paying wages to more motivated freemen became slight. When this point of no significant difference between the cost of slaves and the cost of freemen was reached, slavery became even more economically retrogressive because the slaves were not free consumers, while wage-earners constituted a population who could become the basis of new and expanding consumer markets. Slaves did not constitute such a consumer market because of all the prohibitive laws directed against them at the time.

Perpetual involuntary servitude caused blacks to work carelessly and wastefully. If they made slavery profitable in any way, they would have been working against their own estate interest. With this fact in mind, many blacks gave their labor, as Genovese said, "grudgingly and badly." The result was predictable. Economic progress in the South generally lagged behind the North because production of the gross regional product was purposely undermined from within. The limited output and the abuse of equipment perpetrated by consciously militant and resistant slaves helped in a way to bring down the slave system.

Persistent slave resistance had another economic and political consequence: it gave impetus to the ever-present white antislavery forces which were always looking for evidence to undermine the value of slavery. Moreover, industrialization was creeping into the South after an industrial revolution had already occurred in the North. Immigrants constituting a pool of cheap manual labor made free laborers more and more attractive while simultaneously reducing the attractiveness of slaves, especially resisting slaves. Slave resistance and industrialization helped bring down agrarian slavery.

After the Civil War, blacks shifted their energies and efforts to black assimilationism, to accelerate their participation in the mainstream of the society. As is well known, they became very active in politics and in the economy. A great many black schools were started, as well as a number of black banks. Through banks, blacks were capitalizing for investment in the emergent industrial and commercial development that was occurring in the South. The whole society was industrializing, and most black leaders opted for black advancement within that industrial and commercial system.

Blacks made social progress by increasing their number active in politics and in economic matters. In fact, blacks began assimilating so rapidly that whites who had been used to having the blacks work for them felt threatened. The whites reacted with a resistance movement of their own. They initiated blocking actions to reduce the black advancement in the system, setting about the task of reversing most of the gains that blacks had made. Perhaps they only wanted to slow down some of the infiltration, but they succeeded in nullifying many of the gains that blacks had made. They turned out of office those blacks who were political officials, and they helped see to it that black banks, businesses, and crafts did not survive.

Blacks did not stand idly by and watch their power be taken away. They fought back. The tenant farmers and sharecroppers organized in several states and protested the debt-peonage system and the disfranchisement of blacks. They used nonviolent direct actions such as strikes, boycotts, work disruptions, and other devices. They tried to bargain collectively with whites to preserve some of their gains and to achieve other goals which would have been attained except for white restriction. Mass strikes and mass resistance of other types were all they could do at this time. But the black codes and jim-crow police tactics and terrorism were overbearing.

Even though the society was changing, this oppressive situation did not change radically until World War I. Prior to that time, immigrants were hired in preference to blacks. But when the war started and immigration had slowed so that labor in the industrial North was in demand, blacks were encouraged to leave the South for the industrial centers of the North. The factories of the North were booming. The great incorporation movement had occurred and the mass production of cars and other products was becoming an established feature of the industrial system. Mass production demanded mass labor. The labor demand was so great that there was room for both blacks and immigrants. Thousands upon thousands of blacks answered the call by emigrating from the South to the North. In reaction, whites tried to keep them in the South, even detaining them at train stations, but they kept on pushing North. The North, however, was not as promised, and blacks found new problems there.

The post-WWI period of neo-abolitionism and neo-assimilationism was led by the NAACP and the National Urban League. The NAACP led the abolition of the black codes, and the NUL led assimilation into the mainstream of urban life. In trying to move into the mainstream, blacks found themselves again in the position of having to call on nonviolent direct action to penetrate the system. Some of the actions were against the corporations, taking the form of strikes, boycotts, and collective negotiations. Some of the actions were against the unions, and they took the form of strike breaking. Some of these attacks were against the retail distributors, and these took the form of picketing and sit-ins, and boycotts. During this period of assault, blacks were active on several fronts in their efforts to move into the mainstream and complete the process of emancipation.

The geographical context is now one of urban location, and the economic context is what has been called the new industrial state, consisting of oligopolies, monopolies, and conglomerates. Even the retailing establishments are highly incorporated, usually organized into chain stores. Nonviolent direct action is still effective under these new conditions, and we find that blacks today are attacking two foes in particular: the industrial producers and the chain-store retailers. Blacks have been using strikes, boycotts, pickets, and civil disobedience in order to redress long-standing grievances; they want more jobs in these industries, and they demand retail outlets for the goods produced by black manufactuers and processors. Before this time, black producers have not competed well because they have not been capitalized enough to control or own their own distribution outlets. In order to persuade distributors to accept products produced by blacks they have had to engage in picketing, boycotts, strikes, and other forms of non-violent disruption. Now, with the department stores and supermarkets serving as their outlets, blacks are in a much better competitive position.

In this post-1965 era of black separatism, blacks are using many of the same strategies as before, but what is new is the attempt to develop separate parallel institutions to those of the whites. During the neo-abolition and neo-assimilation phase, the blacks were trying only to integrate with whites. Now blacks are trying to build up their own factories and produce their own products. They are trying to develop the local community institutions as a black entity. The black separatists are in fact trying to gain access to the capital means and the retail outlets which will make black producers and processors viable. In time, they hope to set up their own retail outlets, giving blacks substantial control over the means of both production and distribution in black communities across the nation. Separate development is the ethos of the day.

Emigration
Blacks have long considered the thought of moving away from whites. When they could not move against them or toward them, blacks have sought to move away from their oppressors not only on a regional basis but also on a national basis.

From the time they were brought here on slave ships, the strategy of flight has been imprinted heavily on their minds. Many blacks jumped ship and fled rather than become perpetual servants, while other blacks after landing chose to risk capture and death at the hands of Indians rather than remain in bondage.

Thousands of slaves (perhaps 50,000) who could not see the efficacy of violent rebellion fled the southern plantations and the northern towns where they were enslaved during the time of the black abolitionism. More blacks attained freedom through flight than through any other method, making emigration the most successful strategy of black liberation. Tens of thousands of advertisements for runaway slaves appeared in southern newspapers.

The strategies for escape were both individual and collective. Both worked well. The best-organized strategy of this variety was the Under-Ground Railroad, which constituted a type of guerrilla organization of blacks and whites strung out across the nation from the deep South all the way to Canada. This secret organization was made up of numerous escaped slaves and white abolitionists. Having escaped themselves, former slaves would aid and abet other blacks in their attempts to escape from perpetual servitude by leading them through woods and swamps to the free territories of the United States.

Like all other tactics, this one had damaging effects on the racist system; naturally the Whites sought to stop it. One by one the various states passed fugitive-slave laws, and even the federal government intervened legislatively to help the slave owners and slave catchers. The federal legislation called for stiff penalties for those who aided and abetted fugitive slaves, and provided for lucrative rewards for those who recaptured the runaway blacks. Despite the odds, brave black men and women defied all these machinations and struck out for freedom through flight with the assistance of the Underground Railroad.

Fugitive slaves were one of the most important control problems, and thus elaborate preventive systems were organized and established to keep slaves from running away. Simultaneously, elaborate retrieval systems were developed to hunt down and bring back fugitives. When there were no free territories to which slaves could run or when these areas were impossible to reach, blacks ran away to forests and swamps and lived as maroons rather than as slaves. Flight was effective not only because it denied the slave master a productive laborer, but also because it signaled that a potential guerrilla warrior was loose in the territory. Emigration became a means of liberation because "He who runs away will fight on another day." Some of the greatest abolitionist leaders had been runaway slaves, and as such, clearly symbolized in the minds of other blacks that running away could lead to liberation. Blacks all during slavery continued to leave the South and move to nonslaveholding states just before the Civil War. Even though many of these states had passed laws during slavery to prohibit runaway slaves from entering and settling, blacks moved into them when possible. Many had been prohibited from taking up residence by various legal measures and racist practices.

The idea that social and economic conditions were a little better in nonslaveholding states was widespread all during the time of slavery, because all during slavery, especially during the first half of the nineteenth century, freed blacks and fugitive blacks held regional and national conventions in free states to discuss and to map strategies for the liberation of all blacks. These conventions served to support the contention that there were more opportunities for blacks emigrating to nonslaveholding states. Many of these black conventioneers had become themselves symbols of what social, economic, educational, and political opportunities could do for slaves who aspired to be free. The hopes and ideals of these free men were disseminated by various periodicals and journals published by those active in the abolition movement, and, during black assimilationism, those who were freed were indeed attempting to emigrate from what were known as the slave states. But there were laws prohibiting the free movement of blacks in most states at the time.

Consequently, after a federal fugitive-slave law was passed about 1850, freed blacks and fugitive slaves held several national conventions for several consecutive years to explore the possibilities of emigrating en masse from the United States. As the federal government got more and more into the fugitive-slave-catching business by passing more supportive legislation and setting up the formal machinery for enforcing the laws, many freed blacks interpreted these actions as a sign that they too could be reenslaved. Many became doubtful about their chances for abolishing slavery and for their eventual social and political assimilation into the mainstream of American life. They thereupon decided that they had to get busy and work out some means for emigrating to Africa and/or some of the Caribbean Islands. Still other plans were made for emigrating to Canada as another possible alternative. Several hundreds left the U.S. during this time.

After the Emancipation Proclamation, the motives and reasons for emigration changed, but the importance of emigrating to Africa was kept alive by various black nationalists during periods of black assimilationism. After the black codes and the jim-crow system became fully operative, the black nationalists were able to build on the resentments of a large number of blacks and make a strong bid for national emigration. Bishop Henry Turner was one of the great black nationlist leaders of this movement around the turn of this century, when two or more shiploads of blacks did leave for Liberia. Other blacks in large numbers, desiring to leave the United States, began saving their money to pay their passage to Africa, but later were defrauded of their money by white and black opportunity-seekers who capitalized on their helpless desperation.

The idea of emigration remained very salient during the time of neo-abolitionism and neo-assimilationism. Thousands of blacks emigrated from the South to the North in search of a new homeland and a new set of economic and social opportunities for advancement. They had been encouraged to do so by both white and black recruiters who came to the South, telling of great opportunities for industrial and social advancement in the North. Consequently, thousands of blacks emigrated and crowded into the urban centers of the North. They, however, soon found themselves completely immersed in poverty and slums and the idea of emigration to Africa became attractive again as a good strategy for overcoming disappointment and economic deprivation in the U.S. Blacks were already in the mood to move and to advance themselves, as represented by their emigration North and in their goals upon arriving there. They needed only a charismatic leader like Marcus Garvey to turn their feelings and aspirations into acts toward some organizational and material ends. So Marcus Garvey's back-to-Africa movement blossomed for a short time during the early 1920's. The movement collected money, started several black businesses, started a ship line, and made tentative arrangements for settlement of blacks with officials of Liberia. But this goal was not to be realized. The white supremacists frustrated the movement by arresting Marcus Garvey and causing Liberian officials to withdraw their offer. The whites stopped the man but not the emigrationist sentiment. Perhaps withdrawal of Liberian commitments did more than anything to stop the back-to-Africa part of the Garvey movement.

More recently, under the sway of black separatism, black separatists have rekindled this sentiment which has laid dormant for a generation, and revitalized it with several new initiatives. Some emigrationists are calling for emigration from white-dominated residential areas to black urban ghettos. Others are calling for emigration from the United States to selected African countries. At least one separatist organization is calling for emigration from the northern cities back to the southeastern states where most blacks originated and where the great majority of those blacks outside the North still reside. As black genocide becomes more and more apparent in the United States, the emigrationists of the black separatist movement will be coming more credible among the leadership of Afro-Americans. Their proposal will seem more and more plausible.

Looking back, it is clear that emigration has been a continuous consideration in the blacks' struggle for liberation. There is a long tradition of perceiving freedom in terms of emigration, and a long record of practical applications of this idea, which is still very much alive today. The goals of blacks who advocate this solution are very much the same as they have always been: Emigrationists seek liberation. They seek independence. They seek economic advancement. They seek human dignity. Most important, they seek a nation and self-determination to accomplish these ends.

Education

Another liberation strategy for blacks' liberation has been education. From the early days of slavery blacks have equated educational achievement with liberation. It may be difficult for non-blacks to imagine that education could be a means for liberation, since they generally like to think of education as leading to an economic rather than a political payoff. But for blacks, education was initially oriented toward a political payoff before it had an economic payoff. This tradition has continued up to the present day: many educated blacks have relatively prestigious occupations which have not as much economic as political influence. Some occupations afford little money, but constitute the means of exerting some political clout. A minister is an example of such a person in the black community.

Many black leaders have viewed education as one of the key means for overcoming institutionalized racism. They themselves have used their education in the cause of black liberation. In every epoch, black leaders traditionally have looked beyond economic rewards to political benefits. In all probability, this tradition goes all the way back to the time when conversion to Christianity was a rite of passage from slavery. Blacks submitted to religious instruction (education) in order to gain their freedom. Education was one of the few institutionalized means for liberation, and blacks discovered and used it until whites passed laws shutting off that avenue. Nevertheless, the connection between education and liberation was not lost. Blacks still sought education by any means possible—stealth, bribery, imitation, or self-instruction. When it was against the law to teach blacks to read and write, come blacks educated themselves. Reading and writing meant to a slave that he could at least gain more access to the *means* of liberation: the courts, the riverboats, railroads, or the antislavery literature of the abolitionists. Literate blacks became a major threat to the slavocracy, and the slavocrats sought to prevent literacy among even freed blacks; they sought to prevent those already educated from mingling with slaves. Even for the white man, education had connotations of liberation.

During the black abolitionism period, former slaves, like Frederick Douglass and Henry Highland Garnet, educated themselves and became forceful abolitionists. They used their education and their position to achieve positions from which to launch their attacks on the slavocracy. They were two among many who used education as a tool for liberation.

Education during slavery was principally religious instruction, but blacks turned it into an institutionalized means for upward mobility. Betterment through education was carried further to include the establishment of underground schools by free blacks for themselves. These blacks set·up their own schools to teach themselves and the fugitive slave who could steal away at night. Formal schools for blacks were later set up by liberal white religious sects like the Quakers. They were basically catechism schools and were oriented to religious instruction. For example, "A school for Negro slaves was opened in 1704 by Elias Neau, a native of France and a Catechist . . . ."[9]

Education for blacks was largely intermittent and subterranean. White owners discouraged it by violent practices and outlawed it by harsh legislation. Whites most certainly knew that blacks were capable of teaching and learning, and with learning they would want to supersede not only shiftless whites but also many competent ones.

A case in point is the slavocrats attempts to miseducate blacks by requiring their attendance at religious instruction. But the slaveocrats, made a mistake. By giving blacks religious instruction, they were nevertheless giving mental training and thus unwittingly developing the mental processes of the slaves. Through such instruction, blacks eventually developed language skills, political ideologies, and social values appropriate to the New World. Upon discovering the value of learning itself, many of these slaves slipped away on their own to read and to write what they found in the Bible, the only printed material available to them. Learned blacks led most revolts.

Slaves in cities, however, had even more learning opportunities than others, with the availability of newspapers, journals, books, and printed signs as well as other written material. Some learned by themselves to read and to write by studying these materials. Those who had learned the rudiments often clandestinely taught other black brothers and sisters what they had learned.

Free blacks in some cities sometimes established formal schools for themselves, and large numbers of slaves would sneak away from their masters to attend. No one knows how many blacks learned to read and write in these underground day schools and Sunday schools but we do know that a large number of urban blacks were taught in this way.

Those who did not have these opportunities took advantage of other means. Like Frederick Douglass, many bribed their white playmates to teach them what they had learned in their white-only schools. Still other slaves learned by imitating their white co-workers on the job. Finally, on rare occasions, some slaves were sent to special schools for craftsmen to learn trades or arts in order to bring in more income when their masters hired them out to others for wages. Once the skills were learned, the slaves used them to produce an independent income, and when they ran away to the North, they were better able to provide for themselves. This is just one more reason why masters considered education dangerous.

During black assimilationism, education became even more important. All major spokesmen for blacks advocated education as a means of economic development and eventual social equality. Booker T. Washington, the greatest leader of this period, advocated industrial and business education as a means of attaining social equality. He believed that political racism would erode in the face of highly skilled and highly trained blacks. He believed this so firmly that he stressed educational attainment exclusive of political agitation. Blacks responded by enrolling in vast numbers in schools set up especially for blacks. Education was thought of chiefly as a means of assimilation, but assimilation itself was believed a step toward eventual liberation. Thousands of schools were started for blacks, and they enrolled in large number almost overnight. Besides elementary and secondary schools begun during this period, Fisk University, Atlanta University, and Howard University were started as well. Since that time, the great majority of black college graduates have come from these black schools and others like them. Certainly most of the greatest leaders have come from these institutions, which is testimony to the liberating effects of education for black Americans.

In the neo-abolitionism and neo-assimilationism period, education shifted as the economic and demographic scene changed. Integrationist blacks were mostly concerned with integrating into white schools at all levels, and thus agitated to force whites to accept them at these formerly all-white institutions. Liberation was equated with integration. Blacks saw integration as a means to a quality education and as a means to more opportunity in the labor marketplace. Since whites had not accepted the legitimacy of the education given in most black institutions, blacks sought to gain credibility and acceptance in white institutions and they agitated for school integration. The idea of liberation was latent but nevertheless present. More penetration in white educational institutions generally opens more doors for other blacks. Educated blacks have been made to feel morally obligated to pursue political ends along with economic ends. They have been encouraged to do so, and chastised when they did not recognize the political significance of their education. A very large number of blacks with college degrees have in fact used their education in the cause of litigation and legislation, which is more testimony to the efficacy of education for liberation.

The black separatists see education as liberating, too. They disagree, however, that blacks can receive the type of education which could lead to liberation if white institutions are doing the educating. They therefore insist on black schools and black-oriented curricula in order to instruct blacks in how to build up their own communities and overcome rampant institutional racism. This orientation has led to the advocacy of separate black schools—black-controlled, black-dominated, and black-staffed. This ideology has led some blacks to set up private schools for blacks only, and has given rise to the black-studies movement in higher education, where the black experience is taught in white schools by those of African descent.

For blacks the ends of education have been relatively consistent. The economic payoff has been taken for granted in most cases, as what blacks have done is to give rise to and perpetuate an ethic which perceives, advocates, and makes education a political instrument in the liberation struggle. This can be accomplished either through attaining a position within the system which becomes a vantage point to attack the system, or through using formally learned skills, and knowledge for propagandizing, politicizing, and radicalizing the black masses who then will move against the system themselves.

Economic Betterment

In the three hundred years that black people in America have been struggling for liberation, they have developed a long tradition of equating economic advancement with liberation. Just as they have perceived education as having such political consequences, they have perceived economic advancement in similar terms. This is not to say that they have not sought economic advancement simply for economic gain, but it is to say that they have looked beyond economic gain to other consequences. The situation is not unlike that of the early Puritans, who believed that hard work and self-denial would result in religious salvation. Blacks have in a sense worked out their own version of this ethic. It amounts to the belief that hard work and self-denial would lead not only to economic gain, but to political salvation or, in modern terminology, to liberation. Blacks came to hold this ethic during the period of black abolitionism when self-purchase became a means of liberation. Accordingly, it became mandatory for blacks to work hard in developing their skills, to save as much money as possible, and to persist in their labors until such time as they had accumulated enough money for their self-purchase. We must note that blacks were working under a special handicap, namely, that in most cases slaves who were permitted to hire out their own time were permitted to do so only after they had worked a full day for their masters. This required a special dedication and fortitude perhaps unheard of before this period. The Puritans themselves did not have to labor under this handicap. It is unlikely that they had to work double-time in order to achieve salvation. As a result of these imposed circumstances, blacks worked out an ethic and a system of conduct whereby economic development was a means for liberation. Thousands of blacks purchased their own freedom and the freedom of their loved ones.

Many thousands of blacks who had achieved their freedom by contract before servitude was made perpetual and lifelong for blacks became symbols of individual improvement for the others still in slavery. Many had distinguished themselves by becoming landholders, landlords, small merchants, and craftsmen. As freed men, they had more privileges of geographical movement than did the slaves, more opportunities for employment and wealth, and more freedom to marry and start a family. Freed slaves were visible examples of a set of privileges which most slaves could hardly even hope to achieve, but white masters wanted freed blacks to be subject to the same restrictions as slaves, so that slaves would have no cause to envy them. Since freed blacks were kept unequal to whites, many of these freed blacks became agitators against racial discrimination. They were, for that reason, widely despised and feared by the ruling class of whites who practiced racial domination on even freed blacks to force them to leave the local communities to which they belonged, thereby removing a manifest threat to the slave system. They began the jim-crow system in order to accomplish these ends.

The previous tradition of indentured servitude had permitted many free Blacks to become symbols of individual improvement. Generally, white masters, for these reasons, wanted the freed Blacks to be removed geographically or to be subject to the same restrictions as slaves, so that slaves would have no cause to envy them.

Even though freed blacks were not socially equal to whites, they did have more freedom than the slaves: freedom of movement and association and freedom to work, play, worship, learn, buy, sell, and mate. A freed black could achieve the status of wage worker, small merchant, or farmer, depending upon his state of residence. Slaves, however, had more difficulty in achieving anything for themselves. It was especially difficult for the slaves on plantations. A large number of slaves in cities not only lived away from the premises of their masters but also hired themselves out with the obligation of returning a fixed percentage of their earnings to their masters. Within this hiring-out system, some slaves worked extra hours and made as much money for themselves as they had to give their masters. By this process, many of these slaves were finally able to purchase their own freedom, as well as the freedom of their relatives and loved ones. Once freed, they were able to buy and retain some personal property like a cabin and land, and thus were permitted to set up housekeeping for themselves. These men had sufficient freedom to come and go during the day or night without a master's permission.

Over-all, the quality of life of the city slaves was much better than that of the country slaves. City slaves dressed better, ate better, and had more social life after their hours of work. These differences were enough to entice enslaved blacks to escape from the country to the cities. Country blacks came to think of the cities as an essential step toward permanent freedom. The degrees of personal freedom were quantitatively different; so were living standards between the plantation slaves and the city slaves. The cities became a great threat to the survival of slavocracy. Urbanization created sociological opportunity for blacks to assault the system of slavery.

Economic advancement was perceived not only by slaves as an act of liberation, but also by freed blacks as a means of liberation from the type of racial discrimination that they experienced. During the abolition period, many freed blacks who had amassed fortunes used some considerable parts of them to advance the cause of their race.

They used the money to litigate in court, to petition the legislature, to travel and speak about the country, and in at least a few cases to help finance emigrations to Africa and to other parts of the world. It was not uncommon for affluent blacks who were freed to use their economic positions and their fortunes to publicize the plight of blacks and to politicize the black masses, who held antislavery sentiments but did not know how to act on them.

Black assimilationism changed the course of economic struggle. With slavery legally abolished, the task that lay before blacks was economic and social equality, advocated, for example, by Booker T. Washington. He suggested that blacks forgo political agitation and concentrate on economic advancement, believing that political equality would come automatically with economic achievement. The idea of liberation was equated with economic progress.

With this in mind, blacks started businesses in great numbers. They started hundreds of banks and other commercial establishments, like insurance companies and grocery stores. A black bourgeoisie emerged. Economic achievement, they believed, would lead to social and political equality with whites, white racism would simply evaporate as whites saw the moral, economic, and social advancement of blacks. Assimilation was for the purpose of liberation, and blacks understood that idea very well.

Neo-abolitionism and neo-assimilationism was a period when blacks started trying to penetrate white institutions and advance within what they called the "mainstream." What they sought was to acquire more positions in the various enterprises and institutions. There was not much emphasis on black-owned businesses or black-controlled institutions. Integration was seen as the means of attaining social and political equality—liberation. Social equality would be tantamount to liberation if it were fully realized, and so blacks tried to gain acceptance within the white-controlled and white-owned institutions in hopes that racism would erode. Integration, then, became the primary means toward equality, an end which was not to be realized. White supremacists rose up to deny blacks full participation and full equality. The failure of integrationism was a rude awakening for many blacks.

Even though whites dashed the hopes held by assimilationists, they did not eliminate the ends toward which blacks were striving, and the goals were clearly political and social. When many blacks discovered that they could not attain their political ends because of tokenism, that is, because whites control integration, these blacks shifted ideologically to black separatism. Black separatism suggested changes in the means of economic betterment but not the ultimate goal of liberation. The new means focused primarily on the community betterment as a whole, rather than on the individual betterment. Development of black community institutions is perceived as the most effective way to achieve black liberation. In short, economic development as conceived by black separatism has multiple ends: It is aimed not only at economic gains but also at the political independence and social equality. Their corresponding ends of black culturalism and black nationalism are clearly sociopolitical ends, which are not economic in nature. Black capitalism is itself perceived as a means of liberating the black community from white domination and control and hence is also believed to be an instrument for political and social ends, such as having black communities self-reliant, black-controlled and black-dominated. If black capitalism can succeed in accomplishing these ends, the black culturalists and nationalists would be correct. Black capitalism for the economic enrichment of a few is not liberation, and economic movements must be liberating or they cannot be acceptable to the bulk of the black masses. Estate and caste must be eliminated or their value will be in doubt.

Legislation

Black Americans have been using the legislative process for at least two hundred years, though such strategy was necessarily of limited value because during most of that time blacks could not vote, much less hold elective offices. Blacks were limited to petitioning legislatures, which were composed solely of white men who represented the political interests of white people. The first such recorded petition to a state legislature was in 1760 in Massachusetts.[10] Thereafter "freedom suits" became common. There was one or more nearly every year from that time until 1775.[11] Blacks such as these in Massachusetts petitioned white legislatures again and again in hopes of winning their right to freedom. Freedom was sometimes denied.

One such petition, signed by Lancaster Hill, Prince Hall, and others, in 1777 made the following plea:

"The Petition of a great number of Negroes who are detained in a state of Slavery, in the Bowels of a free & Christian Country—Humbly Shewing—That your Petitioners apprehend that they have, in common with all other Men, a natural & unalienable right to that freedom, which the great Parent of the Universe hath bestowed equally on all Mankind, & which they have never forfeited by any compact or agreement whatever

. . . In imitation of the laudable example of the good People of these States, your Petitioners have long & patiently waited the event of Petition after Petition, by them presented to the Legislative Body of this State, & can not but with grief reflect that their success has been but too similar— They can not but express their astonishment, that it has never been considered, that every principle from which America has acted in the course of her unhappy difficulties with Great-Britain, pleads stronger than a thousand arguments in favor of your Petitioners."—They therefore beg that their petition be considered and that an act of the Legislature be passed "whereby they may be restored to the enjoyment of that freedom which is the natural right of all Men—& their Children (who were born in this land of Liberty) may not be held as Slaves after they arrive at the age of twenty-one Years—So may the Inhabitants of this State (no longer chargeable with the inconsistency of acting, themselves, the part which they condemn and oppose in others) be prospered in their present glorious struggle for Liberty." Signed by Lancaster Hill, Prince Hall, etc. The names of Judge Sergeant and others are inscribed below. Dated Jan. 13, 1777.[12]

This particular petition led to a bill which was defeated. However, a similar petition in Pennsylvania led to a bill which did eventually abolish slavery in that state (1780).

Blacks pushed the abolition of slavery by legislative measures most actively between 1765 and 1774. During this black abolitionism period, blacks presented several petitions to various state legislatures. Their first tendency was to debate and to discuss the black abolitionist legislation and then to table the motion. Eventually, however, various laws gradually phasing out slavery were passed. Several antislavery petitions resulted in laws which either prevented the importation of slaves, prevented the purchasing of slaves, gave freedom to future-born children of slaves, or permitted the manumission of slaves under specific conditions. None of these early laws abolished the slavery already in existence or immediately emancipated existing slaves. The states which were the first to abolish slavery followed the legislative route of first stopping the trading in slaves before emancipating those in slavery.

Connecticut was a case in point:

The first act looking toward abolition was that of 1774, forbidding the importation of slaves "by sea or land, to be disposed of, left, or sold within this colony." Ten years later, in 1784, it was enacted that no negro or mulatto born in the state after March 1 of that year should be held in servitude after arriving at the Age of 25 years, and by act of 1797 the age was reduced to 21 years . . . . So that after 1784 the only slaves for life peculiar to Connecticut were those born prior to that year; and the only other slaves held under Connecticut law were of limited servitude. . . .[13]

Rhode Island, Connecticut, New Jersey, New York, and Pennsylvania eventually began abolishing slavery by legislative acts. These were also the states where black protest movements were most active and where blacks kept petitions before the legislatures. They struggled through white lobbyists and white legal counsels to force recognition of their "natural rights" to be free. By this tactic they kept the pressure on, the debates going, and the discrepancy between American creed and American practice publicly focused.

The presence of this class [freed blacks] prevented slavery from coming to be accepted either by the Negroes or the Whites as a foreordained and necessary institution.[14]

Other states had no intention of following these legislative precedents; therefore, blacks had to devise another legislative tactic for them. Blacks decided to pursue the adoption of constitutional equal-rights clauses, which declare that freedom is an inalienable right of all men; with such constitutional guarantees they could then go to court and sue for freedom from illegal bondage. The result of their efforts and those of others was that such constitutional provisions were the bases for the judicial abolition of slavery in both Vermont and Massachusetts.

In summary, these early legislative assaults were fruitful. With the litigatory efforts, blacks help to abolish slavery for all the then unborn generations of the future in most northern states by 1804. Emancipation of existing northern slaves was not completed by those early acts. The legislative assault on southern slavery was still to reach its peak near the middle of the nineteenth century.

After the American Revolution, blacks were still denied equal education and other rights. Through laws and court decisions slavery was gradually abolished in the North and blacks then petitioned for other civil rights. In 1828 they petitioned in Rhode Island for separate schools. Even before that time blacks in Massachusetts had petitioned for equal school facilities. In 1840 blacks in the same state petitioned for equal access to the public schools. Finally, about 1864, a black organization called the National Equal Rights League was founded to spearhead the drive for political equality.

The second major period of black legislative activity was between 1865 and 1880, the period I call black assimilationism. Through the League and other groups, blacks became highly politicized. This period was the first time a large number of Blacks served in any state or federal legislatures. Most of the southern legislatures had blacks in them, and South Carolina had for a brief time a majority of blacks in its legislature.

> From 1868 through 1887, South Carolina sent 6 Negroes to the U.S. Congress. They were: A. J. DeLarge, Robert Elliot, Robert C. Cain, Robert B. Rainey, R. H. Ransier, and J. H. Smalls. The South Carolina Constitution was adopted by a vote of 60,000 to 2,800. South Carolina was readmitted to the Union. The South Carolina legislature met in July: in the Senate there were 21 whites, 6 of whom were Democrats, and 10 Negroes; in the House there were 46 whites, 14 of whom were Democrats, and 78 Negroes. Francis Cardozo, a Negro, was appointed secretary of state of South Carolina, and served until 1872.[15]

At the national level two blacks served as Senators, and thirteen blacks became Representatives from 1869 to 1876.

The assimilationism period was one of great legislative assaults. After being declared freed from slavery and declared citizens, and after being granted the right to vote, the black masses became legislatively active. The facilitating amendments to the United States Constitution read:

Thirteenth Amendment

Section 1. Neither slavery nor involuntary servitude, except as a punishment for crime whereof the party shall have been duly convicted, shall exist within the United States, or any place subject to their jurisdiction.

Fourteenth Amendment

Section 1. All persons born or naturalized in the United States and subject to the jurisdiction thereof, are citizens of the United States and of the State wherein they reside. No State shall make or enforce any law which shall abridge the privileges or immunities of citizens of the United States; nor shall any State deprive any person of life, liberty, or property, without due process of law: nor deny to any person within its jurisdiction the equal protection of the laws.

Fifteenth Amendment

Section 1. The right of citizens of the United States to vote shall not be denied or abridged by the United States or by any State on account of race, color, or previous condition of servitude.

Blacks now sought to gain social, political, and economic equality. They sought to end segregation and exclusion from education, public accommodations, and court positions. They fought to end restrictions in voting and in participation in the political and judicial life of the country. To these ends, they pressed for and won legislative majorities in some states sufficient to pass supporting legislation. During this brief period, blacks led the passage of some of the most egalitarian laws ever passed in this country. For example, the Civil Rights Act of 1875 guaranteed blacks equal rights to conveyances, theaters, inns, and juries:

Be it enacted by the Senate and House of Representatives of the United States of America in Congress assembled, That all persons within the jurisdiction of the United States shall be entitled to the full and equal enjoyment of the accommodations, advantages, facilities, and privileges of inns, public conveyances on land or water, theaters, and other places of public amusement; subject only to the conditions and limitations established by law, and applicable alike to citizens of every race and color, regardless of any previous condition of servitude.

The civil-rights movement of 1955-1965 was the third period of legislative assault by blacks. It was during the time of neo-abolitionism and neo-assimilationism. During this time blacks were forced to repass legislation which had been passed but was subsequently nullified in one way or another during the Reconstruction Period. From 1957 to 1965 they led the passage of several bills regranting civil rights to blacks which had been nullified. A case in point was the Civil Rights Act of 1964, which forbade discrimination in public accommodations and in employment practices. Examples of these legislative assaults are:

1. In 1955, New Jersey passed a law forbidding racial or religious discrimination in the granting of mortgages.
2. The Civil Rights Act of 1957 concerning voting rights was passed.
3. New York State passed a law prohibiting racial discrimination in the operation of labor-management apprentice programs subsidized by any state agency.
4. Oregon, Washington, Massachusetts, and New Jersey passed laws forbidding discrimination in public housing. The Brown-Issacs bill outlawed discrimination in private housing in New York City, the first such law in the United States.

5. The Landrum-Griffin act authorized Negro workers to sue for the abolition of auxiliary locals.

6. Miscegenation laws were repealed in California, Idaho, and Nevada.

7. California passed a civil-rights bill prohibiting discrimination in business establishments, business and vocational schools, and professional groups. California also passed a law prohibiting discrimination in publicly financed housing.

8. The Civil Rights Act of 1964 forbade discrimination in public accommodations and employment.[16]

These legislative gains it must be noted were made without benefit of significant black representation in either the state or federal legislatures. Public pressure by liberal whites in response to great pressure by militant blacks led to these civil-rights laws. Blacks applied non-violent direct action to produce the crises and test cases which resulted in the passage of these civil-rights bills. These accomplishments assume even greater stature when it is remembered that whites overwhelmingly controlled the legislative houses of all the state governments and the federal government. Whites always had the power and position to alter, delay, nullify, or deny the efforts of blacks. Without power and position, blacks pushed through several major laws which in the main restored civil rights denied during an earlier period. The right to vote and to have equal access to public facilities were prerequisites for accelerated participation in society; blacks opted to move for these gains despite the fact they were not revolutionary. Hence the significance of the Civil Rights Act of 1964 and the Voting Rights Act of 1965 is more far-reaching considered as a stepwise process. Blacks have been trying to influence national policy and consequently have mustered sufficient drives to push through virtually all-white Congresses seven major civil rights bills since 1875, the last six bills coming since 1957.

More recently, during this period of black separatism, blacks have been concerned with legislation which would provide loans to black businessmen, aid to black colleges, and financial assistance to build new black cities or to remodel the present old ones now occupied principally by blacks. Even black power advocates have begun to use the legislation strategy for black community betterment.

Litigation

During the first period of black abolitionism there were great litigatory assaults between 1661 and 1800. The historical record indicates that blacks began petitioning the New York courts as early as 1661. This first petition challenged the legality of slavery (which was recognized in law in the colony at the time). In 1770 a slave in Massachusetts (with the help of other blacks who raise money) brought a successful suit against his master who detained him illegally. Subsequently, in April of 1773, other blacks petitioned the Massachusetts general court for the right to earn money to purchase their freedom. The decision on this petition gave no relief to blacks. Petitions for freedom, however, kept coming to Massachusetts courts and in June some slaves petitioned the courts for both their freedom and land. There is no indication that they were successful. What is significant is that by 1779, both the idea and the practice of petitioning had spread to other parts of New England. Accordingly in 1780 in Massachusetts a number of freed blacks led by Paul Cuffe petitioned for relief from taxation since they were denied privileges of citizenship. Paul Cuffe not only petitioned for relief from taxation but also refused to pay taxes. Finally, taxation without representation was declared wrong as it was then applied to blacks and this approach established a precedent in the struggle for black voting rights. Slavery was finally abolished by judicial decision in Massachusetts in 1783, and in the same year, a second court decision in Massachusetts ruled that blacks were also entitled to rights of suffrage.

Evidently, blacks have found litigation a useful strategy for making stepwise gains in civil rights and liberties. Through the litigation process, using both state and federal courts, blacks have won recognition of their rights to be treated humanely, to have equal protection of the laws, to be witnesses in court, to testify against white persons as well as against black persons, to vote, to hold public offices, to equal taxation, to attend school, and to inherit property—to mention a few examples. Before the formal end of slavery ocurred in many states, blacks—sometimes with the help of a white legal counsel, like John Adams—sued in courts for their individual freedom and won. Through the same litigation process, some of them even succeeded in securing reparations for damages incurred during years of involuntary servitude.

During black assimilationism, blacks were active again in litigation. After the Reconstruction Acts setting up military districts in the South; blacks began to assimilate into institutions, like, for example, education, industry, politics, and commerce. Soon however, nullification began and whites started putting up barriers to assimilation. Throughout the first half of the 1870s, blacks took case after case to the Supreme Court. Almost all the cases dealt with the scope and meaning of the Fourteenth Amendment because whites were trying to institutionalize a "separate but equal" caste system in every area of American life. This struggle layed the basis for the 1885-1900 period of jim crowism.

During the first half of the 1870s, blacks lost most of those local and Supreme Court cases petitioning for equal protection, equal privileges, and immunities. As the court attempts failed, the Civil Rights Act of 1875 was passed to increase the scope and power of the Fourteenth Amendment as interpreted at that time. This act, which provided for equal access to public accommodations of all types, remained in force until 1883, when the Supreme Court declared it unconstitutional.

The forces of white resistance were now in control. In 1895 Homer Plessy, a Black from New Orleans, attempted to ride a white railroad car and was arrested and convicted. The Supreme Court ruled in favor of the "separate but equal" doctrine. This decision set the pattern for almost a whole generation afterwards. This case was as consequential for blacks as was the Dred Scott case.

The Supreme Court in 1899 ruled on three more cases which solidified the superordinate position of whites over blacks. Throughout these years of jim crowism, blacks were pushed back socially, economically, and politically. They were even lynched by the hundreds, and white men and women lynchers went free. Segregation was the watchword of this era.

Blacks would refuse to be denied; they would convene and found organizations; they would plan and propagandize. They would recruit and raise funds for litigation; they would raise up a generation of lawyers to carry on the struggle. They settled on a National Association for the Advancement of Colored People, which was founded in 1909 as an antilynching, antisegregation, and antidiscrimination protest organization.

From its beginning, the NAACP has sought the redress of grievances by litigation. Since its founding, it has pleaded hundreds of cases in order to either win rights or protect the rights of all blacks from various miscarriages of justice. Through the courts, it has opposed the political disfranchisement of blacks as well as segregation in all forms: in residence, education, public accommodations, and the armed forces. It has also opposed racial discrimination of all kinds, especially discrimination in employment practices, medical practices, police practices, and voter-registration practices.

From 1910 to 1960, the time of neo-abolitionism and neo-assimilationism, the NAACP was the spearhead of the legal assault on institutional racism. During this time the association broke down legalized racism in virtually every area of society. For example, in 1935, the state of Maryland had a practice of providing out-of-state scholarships for blacks to attend only out-of-state graduate schools. The practice was declared unconstitutional. In 1937, the association won several court decisions involving equal employment and equal pay for black public-school teachers and administrators. In 1940, through the efforts of the NAACP and others, restrictive covenants in housing contracts were declared by law not binding on home owners who wished to sell their homes to blacks. In 1946, the NAACP won a Supreme Court ruling that invalidated state laws requiring segregation in interstate bus travel. In 1954, the NAACP argued its paramount case before the Supreme Court, namely, the case for school integration. School segregation was declared unconstitutional. This decision was the NAACP's greatest court victory, and since then there have been several decisions declaring various modes of segregation in public accommodations and in public education unconstitutional.

Supreme Court rulings which the NAACP has won have been spectacular. Not quite as spectacular but equally important have been the state-court cases won by the NAACP. The association has reversed many state laws and bureaucratic policies which used to require segregation and subordination of blacks. Practices, for example, of excluding blacks from juries, of extracting confessions from them by force, of segregating blacks within the classrooms of so-called integrated schools, of requiring higher test scores on army intelligence tests for blacks than for whites are just a few which have been overturned through the efforts of this litigation-oriented protest organization. From 1915 to 1967, no less than twenty-one Supreme Court decisions affecting or changing black-white relations have been rendered in favor of black Americans.

Considering the presidents of the United States as the chief legislative leaders of the country who can act within or without Congress, the influence of black Americans on presidents has been notable. Blacks have won six executive orders from five presidents over the past one hundred years. When you consider that blacks constitute about ten percent of the population and only one of the many special interest groups in the United States, six executive orders is quite remarkable.

The present era of black separatism is also one of great litigatory assault. Separatist blacks have not campaigned so much for equal rights as mostly for equal protection and equal application of the laws. They have also been fighting a defensive battle against white resistance movements which have been trying to nullify the wave of black gains over the past few years. The Black Panthers are the best case in point: they are clearly on the defensive militarily and litigiously. Nevertheless, an offensive phase of litigation has begun which is taking the form of class-action lawsuits for damages from past discrimination. Separatists are really after community betterment, and so the litigatory strategy is class-action oriented against both private and public corporations. Community control, community reparations for damages, community development have been the issues of the present litigatory movement.

Blacks in the U.S. have had multiplex problems: estate, class, and caste problems. They have been simultaneously a legal estate, a proletarian class, and a racial caste. In other words, they have been a legal category, all economic forced labor group, and a social status group. It is therefore not surprising that blacks should have used so many strategies for so long a time to overcome their deprivations. As an estate, their rights and privileges were denied by law; as a class, they were economically exploited, and as a caste, they were used and then shunned and segregated at the prerogatives of white people.

Under this multiplex system, individual striving was of limited value. Blacks could individually achieve only up to the legal limits of the racial category's rights and privileges. Hence blacks with high aspirations have been forced into organized actions against categorical discrimination. Without changes in the estate and caste conditions, their individual advancement was impossible. That is to say, class exploitation was perpetuated by means of the estate laws and caste customs. Blacks were therefore forced to rely heavily on the assault strategies of litigation and legislation. As they changed the estate regulations, whites engaging in economic and social exploitation without the protection of law became vulnerable to other direct-action attacks. Clearly then, black reliance on litigation and legislation was justified. The NAACP assaults and victories provided the foundations for other actions, by eliminating legal restrictions on educational achievement, occupational advancement and political activities which were prescribed by law in the U.S. Once these racist laws were made inoperative, some caste norms of discrimination could not stand up under sustained attacks.

The question may be asked: How did the legal norms come to be changed by legislation and litigation? The answer is clear: through agitation, disruption, and destruction. By such acts blacks have pressed liberal white legislators to unbearable limits, and they have capitulated from time to time to the demands of blacks. Once legal concessions were made, educational and economic betterment could move forward with possibilities for more change in the future. Blacks have therefore used all necessary means to change the system of racism in the U.S. Each liberation strategy has contributed to the freedom of blacks, such as it is today. Each strategy has been necessary and purposive. Each, in my opinion, would have been less effective without the others: there is no need to venerate one over another.

5 Organized Black Movements Since 1800

For centuries blacks have wavered back and forth between an assimilationist-integrationist orientation on one hand and a separatist-emigrationist orientation on the other. These two social ideologies have been perpetuated and have been espoused in every historical epoch of the Afro-American experience within the United States. The differences from epoch to epoch have not been radical changes from one to the other, but only temporary shifts in emphasis.

Accordingly, some epochs have been dominated by the assimilationist-integrationist ideologues and others have been dominated by the separatist-emigrationiist ideologues but within each epoch there have been advocates of both positions who were sometimes acquaintances pursuing their respective goals and proselytizing among the masses in order to enlarge their constituencies. There does not seem to have been an epoch in which there were not influential advocates of both traditions. Thus it is not surprising for various sectors of the black estate to be advocating such black power goals as separation and emigration at the same time as integrationism is flourishing. It should not be surprising for some sector of the contemporary black estate to be espousing conflicting ideologies in the forms which they assume today. We have only to look at the long history of freedom fighters like Prince Hall, Henry Garnet, James Holly, Frederick Douglass, Martin Delaney, Booker T. Washington, W. E. B. DuBois, Marcus Garvey, A. Philip Randolph, Martin Luther King, Jr., Whitney Young,

Milton Henry, Stokeley Carmichael, Huey Newton, and Eldridge Cleaver to know that there has been a wide divergence of views among black leaders. Black leaders of all types have been at the forefront of black liberation movements since such movement began in this country. The historical conditions have changed, and with the changing historical conditions the strategies have changed. There is not one typical black response; the black liberation movement responds and adjusts to changing historical conditions.

Blacks seem to have wavered alternatively between assimilation-integration on the one hand and separation-emigration on the other. This is not to say that no members of the black estate have ever entertained the thought of revolution, because they have. Garnet and others called for the violent overthrow of institutional racism during their historical times. In addition, during the Civil War, many blacks thought of the war as a revolution against slavocracy, and whatever their various persuasions at the time the war began, they converted and rushed to join the ranks of those who were in the process of overthrowing slavocracy. We need mention only the names of Delaney, Garnet, and Bishop Turner to document the fact that revolution, given the proper historical setting, is not out of the question for even the black bourgeois leaders. So it would be correct to say that there have been really three basic black responses to institutional racism: assimilation-integration, separation-emigration, and revolution. Most often, blacks have been assimilationist-oriented, but there have been historical periods when assimilation-integration appeared to be unfeasible, so that members of the black estate began to espouse the separation-emigration position.

Changing historical conditions give rise to various kinds of opportunities to assault and change the system. Within every historical epoch, blacks have moved to raise up a cadre of freedom fighters to seize the timely chances for liberation and act on those conditions which invited assault and were open to change. When blacks could not petition the courts and legislatures directly because they were denied the right to vote, hold public office, and bring legal suits, they responded to the condition by cultivating white advocates to litigate and legislate in their behalf. When they could not persuade white advocates to fight for them, they bought their way to freedom through hard work and saving. When they could not even buy their way to freedom through hard work and self-denial, they migrated (ran away) to freedom. And when they could not migrate to freedom, they rebelled and sabotaged in thousands of ways in order to make slavery unprofitable on various plantations, and thereby win their freedom by forcing the owners into bankruptcy. All these responses by blacks have been socially structured, socially determined, socially induced, and socially patterned, and we find that the persons in the forefront of each of these movements have been people from the middle range, people who were just a little above the average in education or occupation or legal situation.

When one looks broadly at the organized black movement in the United States, one can see that in the various epochs they have pursued one or the other of the two basic strategies. For example, between 1660 and 1815 the dominant response of the black leaders was assimilation-integration. To be sure, assimilation and integration were both tied to abolitionism, which was another way of talking about the revolution and overthrow of slavocracy. But about 1815 the separation-emigration ideology suddenly became very strong, and there were voluntary and private attempts at emigration to Africa. About this time, there were also white groups agitating for the colonization of freed blacks in Africa. Moreover, around 1850, after many states had passed fugitive-slave laws, there were great problems with the Underground Railway and the flight of slaves to the North. Consequently, many blacks went beyond advocating migration to the "free" territories to encourage emigration to other places in the world where there were dominant black populations. Some black leaders like James Holly advocated emigration to Haiti. Henry Highland Garnet advocated emigration to Africa, specifically to Liberia. Martin Delaney advocated emigration to the Niger Valley, or specifically to the area now known as Nigeria. Paul Cuffe, a black businessman who had been successful in the shipping business, paid for and took a boatload of blacks to Sierra Leone. But with the exception of these striking personal attempts at separation, the dominant ideology, even during the first half of the nineteenth century, was assimilation-integration.

With the passage of the federal fugitive-slave law, however, many blacks freed and enslaved, became convinced that both assimilation and emigration were in fact futile and that the federal and state governments were laying the groundwork to reenslave even freed blacks. Many blacks who had been freed were indeed reenslaved because the fugitive-slave law permitted white slavocrats to designate any blacks as their long-lost fugitive slaves, and these blacks had very little legal recourse to prove that they were not fugitive slaves. The emigration movement then became very strong, and as a consequence, two or three national emigration conventions were held in the United States at which (expeditions were charted,) studies were made, expeditions were charted and reports published concerning the feasibility of emigration to various parts of the world. However, about 1860 and on toward the advent of the Civil War, many blacks, who had first been assimilationist-integrationist and then separationist-emigrationist, became revolutionists. Seeing the possibility of the violent overthrow of slavocracy, they joined the campaign of the Union Army and petitioned for blacks to fight within the Union Army in order to help overthrow slavocracy. At this point, the bourgeois response shifted because of certain historical possibilities for liberation to a kind of revolutionary ideology.

With the close of the Civil War, the assimilation-integration ideology enjoyed a revival. The era of Reconstruction gave blacks courage and hope that with the demise of slavocracy assimilation-integration was possible. From 1865 to 1880, blacks from the middle range tried diligently to secure government posts, to get elected to public office, to institute government programs of education and economic development for the advancement of black Americans. However, about 1880 after the Compromise of 1876, which provided for the withdrawal of Union troops from the South, the situation again became bleak. The historical conditions became such that the former slavocrats came to power again and effectively began to institute a jim-crow system of debt peonage and political disenfranchisement which deprived the blacks of any effective participation in the political and economic structures.

During this period, from 1880 to 1925, Booker T. Washington was espousing an assimilation-accommodation ideology, or more specifically a kind of pluralism. At the same time, emigration-separation became very salient once again. Bishop Turner, who had been an assimilationist-integrationist up to this time, began actively campaigning and working for the means by which blacks could emigrate to Africa. Several emigration voyages were planned, stock companies were set up, and ships were contracted for during this time; two or three ships did in fact sail for Africa with blacks who desired to colonize Liberia. Between 1916 and 1925, there emerged in the eastern cities, especially in New York City, the Marcus Garvey emigration movement, which constituted the last of the popular black-emigration movements. After 1925, with the rise of the National Association for the Advancement of Colored People, the National Urban League, and some other organizations, assimilation-integration became popular once again and became the dominant bourgeois response.

It has only been since 1965 that another turn in ideology has begun, wherein the dominant response seems to be one of separation-emigration again. There are many, groups advocating one or another form of communal or national separation today; for example, the Congress of Racial Equality and the Republic of New Africa. There is apparently only one group the Afro-American Repatriation Society, based in Philadelphia, which is actively seeking the means by which blacks can emigrate to Africa. I do think, however, it is significant that opinion has shifted again toward the ideology of separation-emigration and that the leaders in this case, as in all the others, tend to be members of the educational, occupational, and financial middle range.

Convention Efforts

Integration

The convention movement of black people for integration began in 1830.[1] It was a collective and organized effort to achieve social, political, and economic equality for enslaved blacks. The representatives to this first convention were delegates of various state organizations. Seven different states were represented. This first national effort met stiff white resistance in the forms of gangsterism and mob violence. Those first brave blacks initially met in secret, but after a few days they met openly even in the face of white threats.

The first convention organized a permanent association entitled "The American Society of Free Persons of Colour, for Improving Their Condition in the United States; for Purchasing Lands; and for the Establishing of a Settlement in Upper Canada." They planned branches in every black community. This new national association was to be nonpartisan and nonsectarian; it was to be oriented toward winning all the due rights and protections for persons of all persuasions. Their weapons were to be "all legal means at their command." In sum, this association was primarily assimilationist in orientation, although it did seek to establish a settlement in Canada. From the beginning, the convention actively resisted the attempts by the white-organized American Colonization Society to send blacks back to Africa. Most black leaders of the day were united in their opposition to this racist group and its degrading, slanderous rhetoric about blacks, and most were united against the society's underhanded attempts to get laws on the books which would gradually strip freed black Americans of all the rights and prerogatives enjoyed by white freemen.

It is important to note that this black-organized, black-dominated, and black-controlled convention antedated the American Anti-Slavery

Society, a white abolitionist movement. In the succeeding years, from 1830 through 1837, an annual national convention was held. After this date local and state conventions were regularly held and national conventions irregularly. The national black leaders worked through the local chapters although the objectives were essentially the same everywhere: to gain civil and political rights and privileges equal to those of whites. This meant advocacy of the abolition of slavery and for full rights and privileges under law for freed blacks. In addition to these legal ends, education, good manners, and morals were established as their betterment goals. The ends toward which blacks strove were both political and social, and the convention movement was the way they chose to achieve these ends.

The national convention movement gave rise to many state and local liberation activities. Free blacks in New Jersey, for example, were encouraged by the conventions to petition for the unconditional emancipation of all blacks and also for the immediate right of suffrage. It was from the stage of the national conventions that Garnet called for the violent overthrow of slavocracy. It was from the stage of the national conventions that Frederick Douglass laid out strategy after strategy by which most black abolitionists proceeded. Encouraged by national conventions, some local and state associations were formed. Some of them organized experimental communities. Others organized task forces to aid runaway slaves; still others started black schools and newspapers; some organized voters; others fought voluntary segregation and intraracial discrimination; and still others engaged in the dissemination of propaganda designed to move apathetic blacks and whites to engage in liberation activities.

The convention movement, both national and local, was perhaps the most important organized effort of the 1830s, 1840s, and 1850s. Conventions were held virtually every year somewhere, and they were the means for the change of strategies which was so vital to success in the liberation struggle of blacks. They also provided a platform for debate and a training ground for learning nonviolent liberation tactics. But the most important product of the convention was the establishment of national and local leadership to fight for black liberation.

Emigration

Going back to Africa has been a concern of blacks from the earliest days. The idea of Africa as a motherland has never faded from black social and political thought. Blacks have debated this issue among themselves for two centuries, and they are still debating it. However, the most notable attempts to translate this ideal into actual behavior and experience began most visibly about 1815, when Paul Cuffe, a New Bedford ship owner, took thirty-eight blacks to Sierra Leone at his own expense. After hearing about it, a number of blacks petitioned to go to Africa, but they had neither the means to pay for their passage nor the means to pay for maintenance in the new land. This outcry for emigration was nevertheless one of many signs of the great discontent among blacks. The fugitive-slave laws of 1850 later added to the number of disenchanted blacks. Many blacks who had believed that integration was a viable course of action began to favor emigration. By 1850 at a national convention, blacks who were previously integrationists were ready to consider emigration as a strategy, especially since Liberia had achieved independence in 1847. Martin R. Delaney and Henry H. Garnet, both integrationists and abolitionists, became ideologues and campaigners for emigration.

The National Emigration Convention of 1854 marked the first national effort by blacks to plan for emigration. The plans published later called for emigration either to Canada, the West Indies, or Central America. The leaders of the convention boldly announced that they were the first black organization to liberate the black man held forcibly in the United States.

On the heels of the Lincoln-Douglas Debates, the Dred Scott decision and the illegal implementation of the fugitive-slave law (which made possible the kidnapping and reenslavement of freed blacks), the leaders of the emigrationist movement began making on-site studies and explorations of various countries, and later drafted concrete plans for emigrating from the United States. Expeditions were sent to Haiti and to Africa, reports were written on the possibilities of success, and aid was solicited from established black and white colonialist groups. Various stock companies were formed to raise money for travel and provisions.

At the third National Emigration Convention in 1858, Delaney's African emigration plans were accepted. At the close of this convention, Henry Highland Garnet established the African Civilization Society to establish in West Africa a black nation of New World Blacks. The African Civilization Society was one of the major black-organized emigration efforts before the Civil War. The society raised money to assist highly select volunteers to settle in Africa. Its political aims were to force the demise of the United States slave trade by colonization and vigorous commerce. It was unalterably opposed to slavery and indentured servitude and considered emigration to Africa as one viable

strategy for undermining these systems. Garnet and the African civilization Society were willing to accept funds from white groups to advance
their cause; others, like Delaney, were not. Garnet also established ties
with African leaders in Liberia, like Edward W. Blyden, and joined his
efforts with those of Blyden to populate that country with blacks from
the United States. James T. Holly emigrated to Haiti with several families. Martin R. Delaney emigrated with others to Canada. Alexander
Crummell took families to Liberia. It has been estimated that more than
20,000 blacks left the United States in this wave of emigration.

In 1861 the Society met in a special meeting. It resolved that the
emigration of all blacks was not their aim. It sought only talented
blacks for the new nation. African nationhood based on self-reliance
and political independence were the basic objectives to be achieved;
thus the society sought only able-bodied black men and women with
skills and knowledge. As the years passed, the activities of this group
became chiefly fund-raising and proselytizing. Since the majority of
blacks resisted strongly any movement to take them back to Africa,
the Society found itself spending a considerable amount of time debating, publicizing, and convincing black people that in Africa there
was a bright future for them. Eventually the Society joined with other
groups to raise funds to promote the colonization of Africa.

Liberation Organizations

National Afro-American League

The NAAL was founded in 1887, before the Niagara Movement
and the NAACP, both of which evolved from the NAAL.[2] T. Thomas
Fortune, an ex-slave, came to New York in 1879 and in a few years
became part-owner and editor of a newspaper, the *Globe,* which later
became the *Freeman.* In 1887 he called for a black organization to
fight for black rights which were denied even under the amended
Constitution. He called for the establishment of a National Afro-American League. The grievances were (1) suppression of voting rights,
(2) mob rule and lynch law, (3) unequal funding of black schools,
(4) convict labor, (5) unequal public accommodations, and (6) denial
of public accommodations.

The principal strategy was to organize in the South, where the
grievances were most blatant. To accomplish the goal of racial equality,
agitation, the ballot, and the courts were to be used. Self-defensive
violence was advocated, but peaceful and lawful means were the guiding principles of the organization.

Local branches of the League were formed in New England, Pennsylvania, New York, Illinois, and Minnesota. In some southern states like Virginia, Texas, and Georgia, leagues were formed. At the 1890 meeting, 141 delegates from 23 states gathered in Chicago. The delegates announced that public opinin, political persuasion, and court action would be their chief tactics.

After this convention, the League began to wane in influence. It had not captured the imagination of blacks. It had not been a grassroots movement. In addition, it could not raise sufficient money to sustain court costs and other campaigns. In 1898, the League floundered from a lack of mass support, but reconstituted itself under the name of the National Afro-American Council. It included the most prominent blacks of the day, but it accomplished little, never having gained the support of the black masses.

Perhaps the most important contribution of the council was to provide an arena where Booker T. Washington, W. E. DuBois, Thomas Fortune, and Monroe Trotter could hammer out what was in the best interests of black Americans. The council kept the various causes and issues alive and helped radicalize and politicize younger men to carry on the tradition. Two organizations soon after evolved: the Niagara Movement and the NAACP. Although Fortune accused DuBois of stealing the declaration of principles from the League, some of Fortune's staff joined the Niagara Movement, which started about 1905. In 1909 the NAACP grew out of this movement, and again former members of the League helped found the new association.

National Association for the Advancement of Colored People

The NAACP emerged to coerce, by legal measures, local and national authorities into extending to blacks their Constitutional rights.[3] The white supremacists had through terror, murder, and miscarriages of justice nullified the implementation of the Thirteenth, Fourteenth, and Fifteenth Amendments. After these amendments were passed, whites rioted against blacks, lynched them, and otherwise physically assaulted them for purposes of intimidation. Blacks requested but received little protection and assistance from white-supremacist governments and police forces. Upon this foundation, the NAACP pledged to agitate for equal rights (political, economic, and educational), to end segregation in public accommodations, to provide protection from violence and intimidation, and to secure strict enforcement of the Fourteenth and Fifteenth Amendments. Furthermore, the association pledged to use all legal means possible, both nonviolent resistance and litigation, to achieve these ends.

Near the turn of the century, in 1909, the NAACP thus became the chief instrument for bringing about congressional action, presidential action, and municipal action against racial discrimination and mal-treatment of black citizens. Leaders of the association intervened in strikes, organized national lobbies, propagandized through the mass media, and sought court actions to end racial discrimination and prej-udice against blacks. Since that time, the Association has waged a pe-rennial fight for fair employment practices, equal education, open housing, free suffrage, equal public accommodations, fair trials, racially representative juries, and equal protection from mob violence and intimidation. It has achieved gains on all fronts. With all these tasks before it, NAACP has been the most effective black organization in the three-centuries-old struggle for liberation.

The NAACP has pursued hundreds of court cases at all levels. It has saved thousands of blacks from miscarriages of justice in the courts. The Association has fought and won cases dealing with police brutal-ity, voting rights, public accommodations, residential segregation, unequal and cruel punishments by courts, and job discrimination, to mention only a few. The most notable victories have been before the Supreme Court: in 1944, against white primaries; in 1954, against school segregation; and in 1957, against gerrymandering by race. It should be noted that during the direct-action protests of the early 1960's, the NAACP was the legal representative for protesters in hun-dreds of arrests. It pursued some of the cases all the way to the Supreme Court and won acquittals for many protesters.

Like all other approaches, betterment through better laws has its limitations. For one, the laws have been good only insofar as the rights and privileges they granted could be enjoyed without fear of reprisal. But since blacks have always been dependent upon whites for the impartial enforcement of laws, court decisions, government policies, and corporate regulations, they have not always enjoyed the full benefits of such legislation. Whites have shown a tendency not to enforce any laws or policies which were contrary to their immediate interests. Thus the greatest limitation of the NAACP program has been its tendency to force changes in legal rules but not in daily prac-tices. Whites have for so long enjoyed the privilege of not complying with the laws that they now have trouble taking seriously any legal rules in the area of civil rights. Consequently, there has sometimes been considerable time lag between the changes in laws and the blacks' concrete enjoyment of the legal privileges or rights. Whites have, most of the time, nullified to some extent the intended effects of the legal changes the NAACP has brought about.

Nevertheless, the efforts of the NAACP have given blacks considerably more opportunities and more maneuvering room for attacking the various racially discriminatory structures and institutions. In addition, the Association has helped neutralize the strategies of white racists. Many times the white racists have been forced to retreat and have had to resort to alternative strategies to slow down the black assault on their racist institutions. The time it has taken them to change strategies and implement new ones has been time gained by blacks in their drive to abolish racism—both ideological and structural.

National Urban League

The Urban League was organized in 1910 and incorporated in 1913. It represented a combination of three other groups: the Committee on Urban Conditions among Negroes, the National League for the Protection of Colored Women, and the Committee on Industrial Conditions of Negroes in New York.[4] It was established in order to improve the lot of blacks living in cities, and has been striving particularly to improve the living and working conditions of blacks. From the beginning it has been an economic-and-social-betterment organization for blacks, and it has been staffed and financed by both whites and blacks. The "vision of social work" and the belief in "justice and fair play in dealings of men with each other" are guiding ideologies of the League. The organization has focused only on the cities where the black populations are large, but it is a national organization with branches in all parts of the United States. White philanthropists, business corporations, and private charities supply most of the financial support of the League. White contributors and white businessmen and professionals make up a large proportion of board members on both the national and local levels. Since its founding, it has tried to establish close alliances with business establishments. White businessmen sit on the local and national boards and help finance the various chapters. Generally, the Urban League has not been a direct-action protest group or a litigation group. It has always maintained that it was a "professionally structured" agency—a social-work agency. It has been chiefly oriented toward solving economic problems, especially the lack of jobs for blacks. In addition, various chapters have been concerned at one time or other with promoting day nurseries, clinics, job training, health education, correction of criminals, legal aid, open housing, public education, vocational guidance, trade unionism, and public welfare. But because of its overriding concern with job opportunities, the League has been closely allied with trade unionism.

In 1963 during the height of the civil-rights movement, the National

Urban League expanded its stated emphases to include racial equality, betterment in housing, health, welfare, education, and employment. It planned to achieve all these ends through expanded alliances with corporations, foundations, and political leaders.

The League uses social-work methods and programs to achieve its ends. As a rule, it does not picket, demonstrate, boycott, sit-in, disrupt, or litigate as regular modes of achieving ends. Its chief methods are moral suasion, conciliation, negotiation, advice-giving, pressure, lecture, propagandizing, agitation, and education. Ideally, the League's leadership would train, educate, and equip blacks to take advantage of expanded economic, educational, and social opportunities in order to achieve a wholesome life in an America which is truly democratic.

The National Urban League is a very important instrument for the betterment of black life in the U.S. The League is about the business of the unfinished Reconstruction which was deflected and thrown off course by the forces behind jim crowism, and debt and wage peonage. Through its employment, educational, housing, and health programs, it is helping thousands of blacks and other poor people to take advantage of the new opportunities resulting from the changes in legal norms. It is community-building time and individual-improvement time and the League is pressing on rapidly in these areas.

Universal Negro Improvement Association

The UNIA was started by Marcus Garvey, a Jamaican who came to Harlem in 1916 after traveling in Europe and Africa, where he found black people all over the world under the control of whites.[5] He decided to unite black people in the common cause of Pan-Africanism. His economic program was black cooperativism, and his political program was national separatism.

The chief strategies of the UNIA were propagandizing and business development. Garvey used campaigns, rallies, and public parades to raise money for various business enterprises. With the money, he bought ships and started laundries, grocery stores, restaurants, and other businesses. These economic ventures were to be the financial means of achieving national separatism for black Americans.

As a volatile national separatist, Garvey strove not only to achieve national separation but also to maintain the racial purity of blacks. Life, liberty, and freedom from white oppression were his ultimate goals for all black Americans and black people everywhere. He believed Africa should be only for those of African ancestry, and he strove to develop among blacks who concurred in this belief the will, the means, and the programs to take them back to Africa.

His chief opponents were integrationists-assimilationists. He was a threat to those who wanted to stay in America and wait for whites to act equitably, justly, humanely, and sanely. Garvey believed that only a black nation was worth all the effort required to build the kind of nation envisioned by the integrationists.

He thought that to contend with whites, compromise with them, conciliate with them, and litigate against them were futile efforts. Whites were not worth the effort. The land, the economy, the capital were all in the hands of whites, who were not about to relinquish any significant portion. To expect justice from whites was, to Garvey, mere self-deception. "There is no justice but strength," he said.

In 1921, Garvey announced the formation of an African republic and declared himself provisional president. He started a church called the African Orthodox Church; God, Jesus, the Virgin Mary, and others were black. He legitimized blackness as a positive attribute. In short, the UNIA was a movement for black economic betterment, black culturalism, black nationalism, black organizationism, and black chauvinism.

National Negro Congress

The NNC, a federation of associations, was organized in 1935.[6] It was an outgrowth of the Joint Committee on National Recovery and of several black and interracial organizations. The organization represented the total range of types and persuasions: parties, fraternities, unions, social clubs, churches, associations, "societies," and so on. From the beginning, with A. Philip Randolph as its first president, the NNC adopted a broad black-advancement program. Over 817 delegates from 585 organizations attended the first convention. In 1935 the NNC called for unionization of blacks, desegregation of public accommodations and schools, protection of farm workers, and anti-lynching legislation because at this time in the midst of the depression, blacks were in a desperate condition. Hunger and poverty plagued blacks in all parts of the nation. Political disfranchisement was nearly complete in the South. Segregation and jim crowism were in force all over America. The NNC thus called for all black organizations to unite and carry out a unified struggle. It organized local chapters all over the United States, some of which functioned even after 1940. The movement was antiwar, and supported civil rights, farmers, consumers, and industrial workers. Politically it was a working-class party.

At the first convention, delegates came from 28 different states. Of the 817 delegates, 743 came from Illinois, Indiana, New York, Michigan, Ohio, Pennsylvania, and Wisconsin. Only 55 of the delegates came from the South. Thus the NNC was largely a northcentral movement, accounting for the great emphasis on workers' causes. The civil rights sector contributed 75 percent of the delegates, but they deferred largely to those representing economic interests.

The NNC dedicated itself to deal comprehensively with conditions facing blacks: low wages, lack of job opportunities, unemployment insurance, lynching, mob violence, police brutality, jury representation, lack of educational opportunities, colonialism, facism, and war. As a united front from 1935 onward, the NNC helped organize factory workers under the Congress of Industrial Organizations (C.I.O.), helped organize farm workers in Virginia, assigned organizers to unionizing laundry workers, and supported the NAACP in its litigation fights. Finally, it actively supported the democratic liberation movements all over the world. Its chief tactics were strikes, direct-action campaigns, mass appeals, freedom rallies, and organizing collective-bargaining groups.

The NNC had a combined membership of over 1,000,000 members. The most prominent members of black America were delegates to several of the conventions. But as the radical left became too influential, many moderate black leaders quit the group. After 1940, its influence among black leaders declined.

Congress of Racial Equality

The Congress of Racial Equality (CORE) was founded in 1942 by James Farmer and a group of citizens from Chicago.[7] It was the outgrowth of an interracial organization called the Fellowship of Reconciliation, a Christian pacifist organization. The founders numbered six: four were white and two black. Two were sons of ministers, three were university students, one was a member of the NAACP Youth Council.

These young pacifists believed in the Gandhian technique and philosophy of nonviolent direct action. Most had a history of pacifist activities and pacifist commitments before founding CORE. Most had ideological preferences for industrial unionism and socialism. Their first campaign as members of CORE was nonviolent direct action against residential segregation in the Woodlawn and Hyde Park areas of Chicago. Their second nonviolent campaign was directed against the exclusion of blacks from a privately owned roller-skating rink.

CORE thus started out as an interracial, sectarian-like organization whose members were required to be committed in practice to nonviolence. Most were also committed philosophically to Gandhian methods, thereby joining pacificism with interracialism, (the elements of the) "universal community."

In the spring of 1943, CORE successfully completed a sit-in campaign against a Chicago restaurant which denied service to blacks. From this early start, CORE began to organize nationally. It remained primarily a small northern organization throughout the 1940s and 1950s. Its principal focus has been equality in public accommodation, housing, and employment.

Quite suddenly in the early 1960s it achieved national prominence. In 1961, CORE initiated a campaign to desegregate interstate buses. The "freedom riders," as they were called, were attempting to achieve compliance with the integration orders issued to the bus companies by the Interstate Commerce Commission. As they crossed the South, they were mobbed, beaten, and sometimes arrested. At Jackson, Mississippi, a bus ridden by members of CORE was burned, and several members of CORE were beaten. For this effort, these brave young militant pacifists engendered widespread respect and sympathy. CORE's image as a freedom-fighting organization soared, and thus CORE became a major civil-rights organization. Through the freedom-ride campaign, scores of business establishments were desegregated. Hundreds of cities throughout the South, where bus terminals had previously been segregated, were desegregated by blacks. Combining other tactics with the freedom ride, blacks from Chicago to New Orleans organized CORE chapters and employed boycotts, picketing, sit-ins, and other means to desegregate all types of public accommodations. CORE's stated end was an open society of freedom where people would be accepted for what they are worth.

Sit-ins and nonviolence became unpopular among blacks, especially in the North. The ghettos were not helped much by the civil-rights gains of the past decade, so in 1965, in response to the sentiments of the ghetto, CORE began to shift its philosophy and tactics. It revised its constitutional prohibition on partisan political action and began organizing the black ghettos. The point of departure was twofold: (1) community organization and (2) political organization. These objectives first meant making the black community aware of its own potentialities to change the conditions which oppressed it; second, they meant organizing the community into a political-action group. CORE used political actions as the chief means to achieve an open society free of legalized race discrimination, segregation, poverty, unemployment, substandard housing, and substandard education.

However, in 1966, under the leadership of Floyd McKissick, CORE endorsed "black power" as an ideological position. McKissick advocated organizing the black community for the purpose of promoting the total advancement of black people as black people.

To CORE, black power meant black political power, economic power, consumer power, pride, legal justice, and leadership. Under McKissick, CORE moved toward open advocacy of black-community control over those conditions and institutions affecting black people. Black separatism through political action was CORE's new mode of seeking these ends. It was called "community self-determination," which referred to the building of black community institutions under black leadership and control. It meant working for racial pluralism in contrast to racial integrationism which meant black individuals getting lost in a sea of white people.

Southern Christian Leadership Conference and Student Non-Violent Coordinating Committee

What has come to be called the "civil-rights movement" began in 1955 with the Montgomery bus boycott.[8] The movement was set off by the arrest of Mrs. Rosa Parks, a black seamstress, who refused to give her bus seat to a white male as was the custom in that city and region. Mrs. Parks was arrested and the black community became indignant.

The idea of boycotting the bus came from members of the Women's Political Council. After a few telephone calls to key ministers, the boycott was agreed upon. The news of the arrest and the impending boycott swept through the black community. The white press publicized it, too. Members of the clergy and of all occupations and professions received calls to meet the next evening at the church of Martin Luther King, Jr. Citizens came en masse. The boycott was confirmed and the civil-rights movement, however localized at this time, was launched. The local movement was spearheaded by the newly organized Montgomery Improvement Association, which carried on the boycott campaign until the white community leaders agreed to desegregate. Thereafter Martin Luther King, Jr., was called to Atlanta to lead a South-wide movement organized as the Southern Christian Leadership Conference. The SCLC was organized in 1957, and Martin Luther King, Jr., was elected its head. It was started by an assemblage of ministers and civil-rights advocates, mostly from the South. It was to be the major spearhead for carrying on the civil-rights struggle for the full citizenship, total equality, and complete integration of America's black citizens. The Montgomery campaign had set off waves of civil-rights protests, and some organ was needed to coordinate the campaigns. The SCLC emerged to fill this need.

It was not until 1960 that the SCLC began to move boldly. It helped organize and sponsor the then nonviolent but militant Student Non-Violent Coordinating Committee.[9] SNCC consisted of delegates from 16 southern states and from Washington, D.C., spurred on by the example of four students.

In 1964 the Congress of the United States passed the Civil Rights Act of 1964. It was the most powerful civil-rights bill to pass the Congress in a century. It should be noted, however, that hundreds of restaurants, hotels, motels, and places of amusement had already been desegregated by the time the bill was passed. The act forbade racial discrimination in public places of business: The bill also guaranteed the legal right to equal public accommodations and to freedom from discrimination in state programs receiving federal aid, in labor unions, in employment, and in voting.

Following the passage of this bill SNCC and the SCLC jointly began a massive march from Selma to Montgomery to climax the voting-rights campaign that SNCC had been waging in Alabama and other southern states. During the protest marches SNCC met with violence from public authorities. Via television, the nation witnessed extreme violence being perpetrated on blacks because they sought to register to vote and because they were protesting the denial of that right. Again, in order to establish peace and order in the streets, the President of the United States called for a voting-rights bill. The bill was to remove some obstacles to registration and to provide protection from violence in the exercise of that right. The Voting Rights Act of 1965 eliminated all qualifying tests which were racially discriminatory and gave bold powers to the Attorney General to provide physical protection and federal registrars if need be. Selma was the setting for the initiation of this legislation. It was a fitting climax to a movement which had begun ten years before and had transformed the South in many ways.

The SCLC and SNCC together either initiated or helped local groups carry out hundreds of sit-ins and marches throughout the South, the first sit-in being at a lunch counter in Greensboro, North Carolina, on February 1, 1960. More than 150 cities were hit by the sweeping wave of nonviolent demonstrations carried out under the leadership of these organizations. As the demonstrations increased, the protest techniques proliferated into kneel-ins, wade-ins, stall-ins, pray-ins, walk-ins, stand-ins, and other imaginative tactics of disruption. North and South, in hundreds of cities and towns, blacks protested against segregated restaurants, hotels, motels, parks, pools, churches, and theaters.

The high point for the SCLC was reached in the Birmingham, Alabama campaign. In April 1963, the SCLC opened a campaign against racial discrimination in public accommodations. It called for the desegregation of lunch counters, restrooms, and other publicly offered accommodations. The association also called for hiring and upgrading blacks in the local business establishments. Later, as more and more protestors were arrested for sitting-in and picketing stores, the SCLC called for the mass release of the arrested demonstrators. The confrontations intensified, and the marching, picketing, and sitting-in increased. The demonstrators were met with violence from white authorities using clubs, dogs, electric prods, bullets, high-pressure water hoses, tear gas, and other weapons. Children were not spared. Federal intervention was forced by the public outcry against official brutality. The President of the United States called for a strong civil-rights bill in order to deter blacks from taking to the streets and disrupting the workaday rhythm in hundreds of communities.

As blacks met with more and more violent resistance from whites, many civil-rights activists after ten years became disenchanted with the demonstration-legislation strategy. It was too slow and it was not providing blacks with the immediate enjoyment of legal rights and safeguards. This deficiency was highlighted when James Meredith tried to walk through Mississippi in the name of peace and freedom and was shot in the back by a white man. This incident prompted many blacks to reverse their ideological stance; it was sufficient cause to justify changing from nonviolent to violent methods. Many young civil-rights activists called for violent retaliation on a mass basis. Others called for a broadly based black Power movement. Racial respect, equality, and betterment were not being achieved through the nonviolent struggle for integration. The blacks in the northern ghettos had not benefited at all from the integration campaigns in the South because they had enjoyed their legal rights for a long time. They were interested in economic betterment and human dignity. The SCLC thus turned its attention to the northern ghettos and began Operation Breadbasket, an economic-betterment campaign for more jobs.

Black Panther Party

Huey P. Newton and Bobby Seale started organizing the Black Panther Party in October, 1966.[10] The goals of the party started out basically those of any group seeking physical and social betterment and security. Their wants were human and simple: education, clothing, justice, and some peace. Peace proved much more difficult to obtain, at least initially, than the other goals. Blacks in Oakland, California, claimed they were constantly and unnecessarily brutalized by the police; so the Black Panther Party set itself up as an instrument of self-defense against this type of brutality.

From the outset, Huey Newton was Minister of Defense, and Bobby Seale was Chairman of the Party. As a party dedicated to black self-defense, the Black Panthers committed themselves to using any means necessary to achieve this end. Realizing that they needed instruments to back up these commitments, they set out to raise money to buy arms. They eventually purchased some shotguns and proceeded to patrol the ghetto of Oakland to protect black citizens from the police brutality which was commonplace. It was during these patrols that the armed confrontations and shoot-outs occurred.

As the months passed, the leaders of the party began to evolve a political ideology to guide the strategies and tactics of the members who were growing in great number in the East Coast cities. In their political analysis, the ghetto is termed an "internal colony," which is unfree, involuntarily unemployed or underemployed, ill-housed, poorly taught by teachers, brutalized by the police, and unequal before the law. Blacks are in a perpetual condition of oppression and exploitation. The Panthers see the United States as a capitalist-racist system of exploitation and oppression which must be overthrown and replaced with democratic socialism if blacks are to have a better life.

Because of the long list of abuses and usurpations, the Panthers declared, as the forefathers of this nation did, that "it is their right, it is their duty, to throw off such government, and provide new guards for their future security." Based on this moral premise, the Panthers dedicated themselves to overthrowing the capitalist and racist power structure of the nation. Thus they declared themselves to be "revolutionary nationalists," in contract to "cultural nationalists," who did not directly pursue political power, but pursued other, nonpolitical ends. As revoluntionaries, the Panthers dedicated themselves to putting an end to black oppression and exploitation. Service, liberation, and revolution became their guidelines for action. Any people black or white who were not engaged in these activities were antirevolutionaries or reactionaries.

The Panthers see themselves as the vanguard of a revolutionary movement. They have set for themselves the tasks of radicalizing and politicizing the black masses by bold, direct actions to demonstrate the means and strategies for resisting the white power structure. They have set out to show how not to be personally "cowed, or intimidated, by death, imprisonment, or exile and continue to develop and expand." In addition to directly standing up to "white oppressors" with superior arms, the Panthers have established some demonstration-betterment programs. The demonstration programs include free breakfast programs for children, free health clinics, free clothing programs, liberation schools, and community centers. These programs are at once demonstrations of collective self-help and self-sufficiency and mechanisms for political indoctrination and party recruitment. Realizing that effective power flows from the people and that the end of all power must be the people, the Panthers have made the "power to the people" their expressed cause. To accomplish a revolution, people must cooperate and that means that they must be educated politically, trained militarily, organized strategically, and led boldly. Building a people's movement is more important than acquiring superweapons or money because the money and weapons are effective if, and only if, the people consent. Win over the people, and the capitalists-racists with the guns and the money will be defeated because all the money and guns the oppressor can muster cannot control a people who refuse to acquiesce.

The Panthers advocate "all power to the people." They have set upon the course of wresting the highly concentrated power from the present power structure and returning it to the people. Huey Newton and the Black Panther Party have pledged them to "true communism" as the ultimate end. The new framework calls for the joining of "revolutionary intercommunalism and communism." This is the ultimate result of "power to the people."

Contemporary Organized Movements Evaluated

Within Afro-American history, the most notable black freedom fighters have been individuals from the "middle range" economically, educationally, and occupationally. The active constituencies of these organizations have also been people mostly from the middle range. Even those movements initiated by the lowest stratum of the black community have ultimately been preempted and thereafter led by people from the middle range; they were the individuals who have had the special skills, knowledge, and performance which were needed to carry out various liberation activities.

Black people have had to use a variety of strategies in order to over-come white despotism, jim crowism, and tokenism. Their weapons for overcoming various forms of institutionalized racism in America have been litigation, legislation, commercialization, education, and bureaucratic administration. In order to effectuate these strategies, black movements have drawn on men and women with special skills, knowledge, and performance and herein lies the primary reason that the liberation movements—the integration movements, the nationalist movements, the migration movements—that is, almost all movements initiated and carried out in this country by black people—have been preempted by the middle class, people from "the middle range" (to use a better term).

Once organizations were established and once they were routinized sufficiently to need administrative-type leaders and technical staffs, those of the middle range were in better positions than the unorganized black masses to carry through new ideas and new strategies in libera-tion. Therefore, the cornerstones of liberation movements were people from the middle range who held privately the very same sentiments as the masses. The leaders of the middle range had the added advantage of having access to those controlling the mass media and to members of the political power structure, which emergent indigenous leaders usually lacked.

The white power structure on the other hand has preferred to deal with the established, even though converted, leaders because they were at least known quantities; their styles, strengths, and weaknesses, were also known. Therefore, the white power structure, faced with probable change, has been more inclined to recognize the legitimacy of the established leaders than that of the new indigenous leaders.

Most often, the new indigenous leaders have been most skillful during the stages of popular excitement and agitation. Rarely have they been individuals who have proven their skills of statesmanship and bureaucratic administration. In fact, at the grass-roots level, many of the indigenous leaders who become prominent during the time of turmoil fail miserably when they are made administrators over implementation programs requiring non-manual and non-verbal skills.

The skills required for legislation, litigation, and commercialization are usually not the same skills required at times of agitation and pop-ular excitement. Hence it is not surprising, sociologically, that the organizational leaders are recruited from a different socioeconomic sector than those who induce the excitement of a new movement.

People in the middle range, with their special skills, knowledge, and performance, not only stand a better chance of rising to leadership within the various organizations, but also, when economic or political opportunities open, are usually the best qualified for the new positions. Within the American social system, position allocation criteria seem to be formal education, work experience, and special technical skills. Obviously, the individuals in the middle range who do not have to go through a lengthy skills-upgrading process, who because of racial discrimination may have for years served as apprentices to whites will be the most prepared, the most capable, and hence the most recruitable for any new economic or political opportunities that open up. And so it is with black movements: the middle-range black-power advocates skilled in economic matters, administration, or community development have the best chances for advancement as opportunities arise. Their skills, knowledge, and performance are more immediately conformable to these new open opportunities, than those skills etc. of the lower socioeconomic individuals.

Those of the middle range have been lately advocating and espousing "black power," in the forms of black culturalism, black organizationalism, black commercialism, black communalism, and black emigrationism. Even though these ideologies are known by other names, such as cultural nationalism, political nationalism, economic nationalism, revolutionary nationalism, and non-revolutionary nationalism, when we examine the most noted existing black protest organizations, we find that almost all of them have been able to accommodate to some feature of the new black-power movement. CORE, once integration-oriented, now advocates black culturalism, black organizationalism, black commercialism, and black communalism. The SCLC and the Urban League, both still integration-oriented, now advocate black culturalism and black commercialism. The NAACP, forever integration-oriented, is beginning to advocate guarded black culturalism. Inasmuch as the new black-power movement has come to encompass so many different facets, it is easy for traditional protest organizations to choose those features which are compatible with what they are already doing and which do not force them to compromise their own long-standing orientations. CORE is a noteworthy exception. Examined closely, each of the black-power doctrines is essentially oriented toward individual or collective betterment *within* the United States. Since the major protest organizations have always been accommodationist betterment organizations, the new black-power movement, which in the main also tends to be oriented toward accommodation and betterment, is, in fact, conformable to the ongoing constituencies within these protest organizations. Each one of these facets—culturalism, organizationalism, commercialism, communalism, and emigrationism—is really an accommodation strategy, so that the protest organizations find that black power as now espoused can be fruitfully incorporated into their present programs.

There is another side to this issue: the white response. We find that the dominant white group has basically three ways of dealing with black movements in this country: co-optation, elimination, and segregation. Let us contrast, for example, the Black Panthers and the NAACP. Clearly, the Black Panthers, at least in terms of their rhetoric, reject both the economic means of the system and Anglo-conformity as a value. To any group that rejects these means and values and tries to substitute others, the dominant white group responds with elimination or destruction. On the other hand, the NAACP, which accepts both the economic means of the system and the values, meets the white response of co-optation. Co-optation leaves them white-dominated, but it does permit them to survive within the context of black subordination and white superordination. SNCC is still a third example: it now rejects the economic means and values and purports to be substituting others; it has met with the same response as the Black Panthers—the machinery of elimination and destruction has been put to work against them. By contrast, the Urban League accepts the economic means and values of the larger society; it has met with the response of co-optation within the context of white domination. CORE, at present, accepts the economic means but rejects Anglo-conformity as a value; the dominant-group response to CORE and to other groups with this particular mind-set is segregation—a kind of containment Finally, the Black Muslims who accept the economic means of the society but reject Anglo-conformity as a value and substitute other values in a nonrevolutionary way, have met with the dominant-group response of segregation which at the present time conforms with the Muslims' policy aims.

Given this set of dominant-group responses which can be brought to bear in reaction to any type of black movement, we find that most present-day black leaders are perhaps accommodationist in orientation, and betterment-oriented rather than revolution-oriented because of the type of response that other actions are likely to evoke from the white power structure.

At the present time, three basic types of black-power activists exist within the black community; nihilists, integrationists, and separatists.

Black-power supporters tend to be either nihilist or separatist in ideology. The nihilists violently reject both the means and values of this Anglo-dominated society and have had the least chance of surviving; we therefore do not find any bourgeois-dominated organizations advocating (at least openly) the nihilist position. The communal separatists substitute black values for Anglo values but accept the political-economic means of the society, and they have usually met with a segregation response by the dominant group. Today in response to separatism, there does seem to be emerging a national policy to contain the blacks within the confines of decaying ghettos and to dominate and control them from the vantage point of segregated communities.

The national separatists reject the values and means of this Anglo society and substitute their own black values and black means. Whites respond passively if blacks simply and quietly emigrate from the U.S., but they respond hostilely with repression or elimination if separatists try to secede from the U.S. Only to the integrationist who accepts the Anglo values and the means do whites respond with a qualified acceptance.

The traditional black protest organizations which subscribe to the black-power ideology have adopted either communal or national separatism. For. example, CORE which was strictly an integrationist organization, has converted to a communal separatist position. Regardless of the position adopted by these latter-day black-power advocates, most have chosen courses of action which do not evoke the white responses of destruction and elimination. To the extent that black values and black means do not evoke the ultimate response of elimination and destruction by the dominant group, the black bourgeoisie, which either leads or supports these various organizations, can find black-power advocacy conformable to their accommodationist and betterment orientation.

6 Black Liberation Strategies Evaluated

Blacks have used a variety of effective strategies to overcome and overthrow white racism in its many institutionalized forms. It is not something new for blacks to advocate "all means necessary" to change the conditions of their existence; they have been doing so for three hundred years.

What remains is for us to evaluate the various strategies in terms of their strengths and weaknesses. All strategies have limitations, but all strategies will work under facilitative conditions, or fail under less than ideal conditions. The best way to evaluate the strategies is to examine the historical record and extract from that record the empirical instances of the various strategies used under varying historical conditions for the past three hundred years. In doing so, we can perhaps discover when and how a strategy is most viable and effective and when and how it is not. Indeed, what we might learn is that the internal arguments among blacks are unwarranted. All strategies are good strategies given the proper historical conditions. Perhaps we will also find out that what blacks ought to be about is studying the conditions and the timing appropriate for the use of various strategies instead of trying to settle on one strategy for all times.

Destruction

Putting aside the issue of whether or not the destruction of persons or property is legal, let us deal with the effects of this strategy. For blacks, destruction of white-owned tools, property, and weapons has been quite effective, especially at times when there have been no non-violent means by which to alleviate their oppressive conditions; violent destruction was necessarily used. The saying that "violence never accomplishes anything" is a fallacy. If your enemy dies for his cause, his death is functional for you. If your forces die for your cause, your enemy can eventually deplete your force and gain victory over you by attrition. Most assuredly violence can be positively functional in many ways, especially material ways.

Historically, the strategy of destruction as used by blacks has had the following main consequences: (1) destruction of white-owned and controlled means of production, (2) disruption of various white activities and institutions, (3) terrorization of white racists, (4) annihilation of white racists.

Sabotaging farm implements and animals has already been mentioned as a key antislavery strategy. Burning stores, factories, and public-transportation conveyances has also been a key strategy. Both of these types of strategies have not only helped to disrupt the normal operations of various communities but they have also had a shock value in attracting attention to black grievances. Terrorism has always marked black-white relations in the United States, and terrorism has been an effective way to neutralize the behavior of the opposition. The fear which follows terrorism has in some instances been as effective in immobilizing the enemy as the act of terrorism itself. Violence can definitely force social changes; if it either defeats, eliminates, immobilizes, disorganizes, neutralizes, or deters the enemy, then violence may be considered effective.

The successful use of violence can have a psychologically energizing effect. When a minority has been oppressed and degraded for centuries, it could develop doubts about its capabilities, and it could lack sufficient confidence that it can succeed in any contest with the oppressor. The minority may even feel inferior and immobilized by what may be termed an "oppression psychosis." Victories through violence often have the effect of raising confidence and generating new aspirations. They can have a resurrecting effect in motivating, stimulating, and activating an oppressed people. Victorious violence, by the oppressed, thus becomes a sign of superior achievement. It becomes self-validating and self-reinforcing to those who need objective victories over their oppressors in order to feel equal, competent, and confident. In short, the suffering of the oppressor becomes redemptive for the minority; it becomes cathartic for the minority and a vindication of their faith in direct action and perseverance.

As it relates to the oppressor, violence can also be an important conversionary force for the oppressor. Oppressors who have been undefeated for years cannot understand humility until they understand defeat. Their supposed superiority will not permit them to see their antagonists as equals or as human beings worthy of human dignity; thus they cannot even sympathize with nonviolent petitions which suggest equality and justice for all. Defeats experienced by the oppressors can make them realize that they are not invincible, infallible, and omniscient. Violent defeat forces on them a consciousness of pain, injustice, inequality, and deprivation. In short, violence visited upon an oppressive dominant group can cause it to be more reasonable, considerate, humble, and conciliatory toward those it has oppressed. In the United States, recent violent victories by minorities have discredited the "hawks" and have given the "doves" a chance to achieve positions of influence and make their conciliatory positions the dominant ones.

Violence can have various consequences for both the perpetrators and their victims. To employ violence effectively, minorities have to decide what ends they want to produce, as opposed to what ends they are capable of producing. The latter capability is more important than the former goals because violence can be counterproductive if it is not carried out in measured steps. Minorities, in assessing their capabilities, must decide whether or not they have the means and the numbers and the materials and to carry out violence of whatever character: reprisal, terrorist, annihilatory, disruptive, coercive, show-of-force, provocative, or insulting. Their purposes and ends must be clear, and their means of attaining those ends must be secured.

One of the counterproductive consequences of initiating a campaign of violence against a dominant enemy is to arouse him to annihilate the minority. This is a clear and present danger in the United States because genocide of racial minorities is in the American tradition. More than once in American history, slave conspiracies caused whites to annihilate blacks in retaliation for insurrections or terrorist activities. The general tendency for whites has been to tolerate very little violence perpetrated by minorities. Even for engaging in nonviolent demonstrations to expose their plight, dramatize their discontent, or seek redress of grievances, racial minorities have received retaliatory blows with electric prodding irons, police clubs, chains, fire hoses, fists, incendiary bombs, dynamite, guns, sticks, and stones. In short, since provocative *nonviolence* has aroused violent white repressive responses, organized provocative *violence* would be even more threatening to whites, who almost always overreact when they are threatened because they feel so much insecurity and guilt about their inhumane treatment of minorities. Minority discontent arouses this guilt and forces the oppressors to face their inhumanity; they retaliate by trying to remove the guilt and those who have raised that guilt to the conscious level. They retaliate so vehemently because they recognize that violent victories by minorities can be intrinsically rewarding. The minorities therefore cannot be permitted to achieve even small successes through violence for dominant-group leaders know that the many U.S. minorities may be aroused to levels of combat which would make them invincible if they were permitted to gather momentum.

Violence, looked at sociologically, can be a unity-producing factor in intragroup relations. Conflict between groups generally has the consequence of establishing internal unity and cohesion within groups. Intergroup conflict pressures nonsolidary persons to come together, producing group unity by forcing the reluctant persons to join the ranks or to go it alone in the face of a hostile enemy. Such conflict also causes petty differences to be set aside or subordinated to the over-all security of the group. It defines very clearly the group membership, ideas, sentiments, and numbers. It makes definitive the actual power relations between two contestants and their bases of power. Conflict within warring groups is reduced; discipline is required, internal opposition suppressed, and coordination increased, making for greater in-group unity and cohesion. Conflict of the intergroup type polarizes combatants, increasing in-group morale and *esprit de corps.*

Contrary to the thinking of many blacks, the author feels that the use of violence by blacks in the U.S. has been positively functional for blacks and for whites. For whites it has dramatized the gravity of the economic and political machinations they have perpetrated on blacks; for blacks it has given them knowledge of the fallibility of the superpowerful white man. Violence has been functional in other ways. While it has not cost whites much in the way of destroyed property or lives, it has cost whites millions of man-hours of work lost during the violent disruptions. It has also cost whites peace and contentment which cannot be had with thousands of angry destructive blacks running around in every major population center where most of the white people play out their everyday lives. This threat of violence is brought into sharp relief as soon as a black Mau Mau or underground guerilla group starts to operate in any of our urban places, and shows that violence can serve purposes no other strategies can serve, and hence ought to be kept as part of the black arsenal to be used when necessary.

Nonviolent Direct Action

Quite often, control over the means of force and violence has been so monopolized by the dominant group that blacks have had a difficult time effectively using violence. Under these conditions nonviolent resistance has sometimes been the only effective option for producing change. Picketing, striking, slowing down, sitting-in, and other such acts have been the key tactics of nonviolent opposition.

This kind of civil disobedience has not been law-breaking for its own sake. Blacks who have acted disobediently have recognized that they could be punished, but they have persisted in order to expose unjust laws and practices. The attendant suffering has been functional; it has dramatized the inhumanity and the injustice of the white man to the black man, and it has pointed out not only how dehumanized the minority can become, but also how dehumanizing the oppressor has already become. Black suffering through disease and deprivation has exposed the pathological and degrading nature of a racist system; cases in point are slavery, slums, poverty, oppression psychosis and crime.

The legacy of nonviolent opposition throughout history has been the achievement of victory out of apparent defeat, at times victory in death, and at other times redemption in suffering. As whites have believed that material and conspicuous achievement in one's calling is a good indication of moral worth, many blacks have been forced to accept an analogous psychology that long and conspicuous suffering in a spirit of love is redemptive. Such blacks have for centuries believed that their sufferings in America would eventually be redemptive, and so they acquiesced to their violent oppressor, suffered all of his indignities, and put up with his dishonorable use of power and privilege. They believed that "right" would triumph over "wrong." In some sense it was a survival strategy, for the alternatives were suicide, infanticide, self-maiming, schizophrenia, and other pathologies.

The logic of nonviolence is that redemption would occur through the conversion of oppressors into liberators. Blacks have thought that by enduring more suffering than the oppressors could perpetrate, sentiments of sympathy and compassion would be aroused in their oppressors and would lead to conversion. This belief was predicated on the assumption that the oppressor had a conscience and saw the suffering blacks as fellow human beings with whom he at some time identified. Quite often, however, the white oppressor defined blacks as subhuman and unworthy of humane treatment, so that feelings of sympathy and compassion were rarely aroused.

Blacks have come to believe that if suffering is redemptive for one, it should be redemptive for the other. That is, suffering on the part of both the minority and the dominant group should be productive. Accordingly at times, blacks have induced suffering on the part of the dominant group. Such suffering has helped point up the gravity of racial discrimination and racial injustice. Such suffering by whites has helped produce increased awareness of their behavior and has helped bring some of them to "right reason," as blacks see it.

Sociologically, nonviolent direct action has also been instructive in that it has pointed up the close interdependence of subordinates and superordinates. Black noncooperation has vividly dramatized just how masters and servants need each other in order to survive. Racial opposition has dramatized the point that both whites and blacks are locked in social relationships in which the cooperation of both must occur or the coexistence cannot continue. In most situations blacks cannot be immediately replaced by immigrants or machines; thus the real interdependency with the dominant group is revealed. The cooperation of blacks is therefore prerequisite for maintaining the effective level of national productivity, stability, and safety.

Slavery, and for that matter any forced-labor system, has thrived on black acquiescence. When there has been a choice between acquiescing or dying, most blacks have chosen to acquiesce. They have chosen to cooperate, however grudgingly, until such time as they could change the system. Such cooperation by blacks helped perpetuate the forced-labor systems—slavery, debt peonage, and wage peonage. While some have chosen death, the great majority have chosen to live under oppression. They have been sustained only by the hope that victory was eventually going to come and that they would be liberated, saved, rescued, or delivered after and because they endured the long suffering.

But hope and faith have not been sufficient. Economic means, geographical location, and social position have been critical for the success of nonviolent direct action. The numerical concentration of blacks in cities has provided a lever for producing significant results when blacks have decided to use nonviolent direct action. Through the strategic location of the black population and through critical timing, mass nonviolent opposition has succeeded and can continue to succeed in the United States.

Litigation

Blacks have been using the strategy of litigation for more than two hundred years. On different occasions, however, they have been denied the right to sue, testify, sit on juries, and hold judgeships. Thus one of the most important means for achieving social change has been denied to blacks. Despite this suppression, blacks never lost sight of the litigatory weapon, knowing that the estate aspects of the system had to be changed in order for there to be a proper historical moment when this strategy could be used.

Without the direct access to the courts, blacks have been forced to develop the indirect approach of "interposition," the act of interposing a third party between the oppressed and the oppressor. Many white abolitionists voluntarily offered themselves to be interposed between the slavocrats and the blacks. By filing court petitions for blacks, testifying in court on their behalf, and propagandizing for them in those situations where blacks were prohibited by law or by custom from acting in their own behalf, interposition became real and effective.

With such allies, blacks have been only moderately successful. Success has been largely dependent upon the political persuasions of the court principals—the witnesses, jurors, judges, and attorneys. Most of the time, such functionaries have been wholly or partially pro-slavery, and thus they have acted negatively on any petitions which would have abolished slavery and would have granted blacks some measure of legal or social equality with whites. Being white, proslavery, and in positions of great power and discretion, such functionaries have usually acted unjustly towards blacks who could do little about it. During most of this time, blacks were not voters, or public officials, or men and women of great economic power. So they had no effective way within the system to neutralize directly the power of racist court principals. Because there has been little effective opposition from blacks, white proslavery court functionaries have been able to withhold from blacks either the immediate enjoyment of their legal rights, or protection from vigilantes acting in violation of the law.

The use of litigation as a strategy has varied from colony to colony and from state to state. But in all instances, blacks have had to win legal recognition of these basic facts that they were citizens of this nation, and specifically, that the constitutional rights which applied to white men also applied to black men, and that blacks had the right to petition, sue, testify, sit on juries, and hold judgeships. As blacks have won legal recognition of these rights, they have been able to use the litigatory strategy more directly and effectively to assault racist institutions. On occasion, they have been able to use the judicial institution as a countervailing power to other institutions that were still pursuing their ends by racist means.

The effective use of litigation has been slow in developing. To use this strategy effectively, blacks have had to develop their legal sophistication by encouraging some of their most talented group members to become highly skilled lawyers. All of this has taken time, but it has been time which had to be taken, for the white adversary has been an able and cunning opponent. It has taken time to acquire the requisite knowledge of court procedures and of writing well-researched briefs. Blacks have had to develop great skill and finesse in order to deal with the white bigots who were the court principals sitting in judgment and rendering decisions on blacks.

All things being equal, the strategy of litigation has been at best a slow and piecemeal way to win rights. But all things have never been equal or even fair, and so blacks have been extremely slow in securing all rights which are enjoyed by other citizens.

In matters of litigation, black lawyers have met repeatedly with failure. They have often failed because of the blatant bigotry of white judges; sometimes they have failed because of their own lack of legal knowledge or competency in court procedure. Blacks have had to "learn the ropes," and while learning, they were bound to lose. Yet in losing, they made gains by learning the legal procedures and knowledge needed for success in battle. It could be said that they were learning the means of victory in the midst of apparent defeat. Through trial and defeat, they have learned the court procedures, the legal research procedures, and the intricacies of the law. In legal combat with a well-schooled adversary, they have learned the most effective strategies and techniques of litigation, and in the end, they have learned how legal change could be initiated and how obedience to these changes could be enforced.

The experience has been long, painful, and harsh, but largely rewarding. Blacks have learned the white man's legal ways, his methods, his *weaknesses*—and the moments to use all of these against him. For example, litigation has been effective because the dominant group has felt obliged to encourage obedience to unpopular court decisions in order to protect the sanctity of future decisions. Whites have espoused a norm of law and order, a society of laws not men. Recognizing this white man's dilemma, blacks have persuaded whites to accept certain court decisions and to obey them, at least until they could be repealed by legal processes. Via this concession, blacks at least have gained time to move against racism on other fronts while decisions are in effect and whites have had to act contrary to their usual racist inclinations. Because they have been obligated "to maintain the law" in order to affirm the integrity and justness of their own legal system, some aspects of institutional racism have been partially eliminated by litigation. Whites have had to put the maintenance of the law and order and the sanctity of the legal system above law-breaking racism.

If we assess the litigatory strategy as a means of ending institutional racism, we must conclude that it has not been a weapon "for all seasons." Like all tactics, it has had its good and bad historical moments. Court victories have often been of limited value because they have been contingent upon the ability of blacks to prevent nullification, delay, and denial of equal protection.

Future gains by blacks rest on their ability to force continued recognition of their claims to legal equality. Blacks cannot take the present recognition of their rights for granted; the enjoyment of these rights requires continuous vigilance. Such vigilance is required because ours is a society of both laws and law implementors. The latter are men and women who interpret the laws according to their own prejudices and cause their interpretations to become law in practice. With such arbitrary discretion continually in the hands of whites only, blacks could lose all their future legal rights and privileges by one or more prejudicial decisions; for example, a decision declaring blacks noncitizens would undo all that has been won in the name of American citizenship.

Court decisions in the past have been made by ordinary men, and such men have been influenced by public opinion. Blacks therefore have to remain aware of the perennial possibility that if they do not command some control over either public opinion or public officials, both of them may turn in an extremely racist direction. Blacks have to remain aware of the racist psychological conditioning, the political interests and the political persuasions of the white men who sit in judgment of their legal petitions. The favorable outcomes of their petitions have in the past been dependent upon the independent philosophies of the men on the benches of the courts. Blacks must continually influence the selection of juries, judges, and other court functionaries, or they will remain forever dependent upon the whims of those dominant-group members who hold these offices, and they will have no success using the litigation strategy. More importantly, they will never be able to guarantee for themselves continued court recognition of their constitutional rights, unless they control to some considerable extent the outcomes of the legal process through controlling the functionaries.

Legislation

Blacks were able to use the legislative process as a strategy to assault racist institutions only after gaining constitutional recognition of this right. As a subordinate estate they were denied these rights by racist laws. Since gaining this right they have had a realistic chance of changing some racist aspects of the social, economic, political, educational, and familial institutions and they have begun to use this strategy more and more in terms of legislation to equalize the estates.

Since whites have written, interpreted, and enforced the federal and state constitutions, they have for the most part prevented blacks by the federal and state constitutions from full participation in the life of the society. Black constitutional rights have not always been a birthright. The so-called "unalienable rights" have not always been enjoyed by blacks, because whites considered them to be "privileges" and white-granted privileges at that. Whites have maintained the control to grant, deny, suspend, delay, or take away these rights. Historically whites have not hesitated to act in all of these ways when they wanted to maintain the political, social, or economic advantages established by their race.

Powerless as blacks have been, the political effectiveness has necessarily been controlled by the dominant group through the contrived processes which the whites have designated as the "political process of the United States." For example, the qualifications for political participation and the degree and nature of that participation have been predetermined and controlled by the dominant group. Whites, therefore, have controlled the degree to which blacks can be politically effective. Blacks have come to live with the fact that without effective control over the legislative process their "rights" could be nullified, suspended, or repealed at any time. Without effective legislative control, the dominant group controls the amount, rate, and even a large measure of the quality of social change in race relationships. Recognizing these facts, blacks have had no other choice but to use the dominant group's legislative process as it exists in order to realize even limited legislative gains. They have had to keep the faith that laws of any kind enacted in the interest of black people have been progressive.

Comparing the legal situations of 1674 with 1974, this faith has been vindicated.

Thus, within certain limits prescribed by the dominant group, blacks themselves have increased their political effectiveness. For example, granted the right to vote when there was a possibility of winning an election, they almost always voted for their own interests, mustered the necessary motivation to promote political leadership, and discovered and used political strategies which would maximize their life-chances. To be sure, they have often lacked the knowledge, money, numbers, and communications media to maximize their political participation and effectiveness. There have always been more opportunities to assault this racist system of ours than could be taken advantage of because the means of assault have not always been available.

Blacks, for example, being numerically small in proportion to the dominant group, have tried to establish interracial coalitions with other small ethnic groups in order to obtain sufficient numerical strength to force the dominant-group legislators to incorporate in their programs some of the interests of the minority groups. When blacks have been outnumbered and clearly without hope of controlling the legislative process alone, it has been in their interest to get some of their members co-opted into the political parties and bodies of the dominant group. In this way, they have, through internal pressure, gotten some of their programs adopted as planks in the dominant group's platform. By this tactic, some of the political interests of the blacks have been legislated into law. To be sure, co-optation has had its limitations. For example, it has divided the energies, financial resources, and political interests of black leaders. Perhaps, for that reason, black leaders of past generations have rarely succeeded in acting exclusively for black people. Instead, they have at times found themselves working at cross purposes with other blacks. That is to say, many black leaders have discovered that they must accept policies which further the interests of the dominant group in exchange for something for their own group. There are costs as well as profits in every coalition.

However limiting the legislative strategy, blacks must still use it to help overcome the white-over-black system. They must recognize that most of their deprivations in life result from racist legal estates begun about 1660. Therefore, even though they are at a disadvantage, they must continue to maximize their political participation in the system to make it work in their behalf. Bad laws have to be met with good laws, and unjust laws with equitable laws. The walls of the legal estate are crumbling.

Although most blacks and whites seem to believe that attitudinal change must precede behavioral change, the opposite is closer to the truth. It is possible to change the attitudes of dominant-group members by legally forcing compulsory changes in their behavior. Therefore, blacks must seek legislative changes. Laws can serve an educational function by instructing white citizens in what they ought to do, in contrast to what they want to do. Laws can serve a moral function by giving white people moral reasons for committing themselves to non-racist courses of action. Laws can have an emotional support function by giving liberal whites legal support for their egalitarian attitudes. Finally, laws can give those white racists who have no desire to change their behavior or their feelings something to fear if they do not change. Thus laws can serve a coercive function by requiring obedience and compelling such people to act contrary to their prejudiced feelings.

Coalition

Conditions considered necessary for effective coalitions will vary from analyst to analyst. Some will mention mutual immediate goals, others will emphasize the same ultimate ends; still others will argue for similar status positions relative to the owners and controllers of the means of economic production and political power; finally, others will stress the same sentiments and beliefs about the opposition parties and the conditions of living.

Let us examine each of these so-called necessary conditions. First, this author would argue that mutual or common goals are desirable, but not necessary. The parties forming a coalition need not have identical goals, but they should have at minimum "complementary and contingent goals." Complementary and contingent goals at least are necessary for the parties to be interlocked. In a contingency relationship, if one party pulls out in order to "go it alone," its goal becomes unattainable. This is to say, when the parties are locked in such a functional relationship, one cannot succeed without the other, and the opposition cannot lure one of the parties out of that coalition into a new one in order to form a new united front against the group left alone. Thus, to avoid such a split, the parties to a coalition ought to have at least complementary goals, the achievement of which involves them in a relationship contingent upon both parties being locked in an interdependent alliance. Since neither party can succeed without the others, there is little or no chance that these coalescing factions will split over concessions made by the opposition to one or the other party to the coalition.

Secondly, the same ultimate ends are both desirable and necessary.

The term "ultimate ends" refers to the pursuit of revolutionary, re-formist, or reactionary ends. Revolutionaries seek transformations of society in terms of new models. Reformists seek transformations of society in terms of present ideals—betterment. Reactionaries seek transformations in terms of preexistent models of society.

Carmichael, Cleaver, and Newton, among others, have claimed that blacks and whites have fundamentally different strategic interests. Whites belong to a privileged estate and have not experienced the racial oppression which blacks have experienced; the racial oppression which white radicals talk about is at most a vicarious experience of black oppression. Most of them do not actually feel the institutions as racially oppressive and exploitative. Since white liberals by and large have had their roots in the economically secure estates and classes, they have actually benefited from the racially exploitative system and have not experienced unjust racial deprivation. Thus, even when whites have great grievances against the system, they rarely seek a racial revolution, but only racial reforms. They do not seek systemic reconstruction, but systemic revision at most.

Moreover, whites have been coercive and exploitative toward blacks. For example, whites using laws and regulations, have structured the housing markets, the labor markets, and the service markets so that they can gain at the expense of blacks; the scarce and overpriced housing market for blacks, the high rates of unemployment and under-employment for blacks, and the lack of public services provided to black neighborhoods are all conditions structured and perpetuated by whites for their own gain. Whites, in short, have built their fortune on the sweat of blacks.

To change this exploitation, whites would have to transfer to blacks some of their monopoly of opportunities for profits, occupa-tional positions, and political decisions. But since most whites wish to maintain their advantages, they strive only to expand the institu-tional arrangements while keeping blacks in their relatively dis-advantageous position. Whites thus seek mere reforms.

It is therefore clear that when black and white parties to a coalition do not define their ultimate ends in similar or complementary ways, one party will then pursue societal models which work against the interests of the other party in the coalition. In a general sense, the parties must agree on whether or not their ultimate ends are to innovate, to better contemporary conditions, or to revert to some previous ideal state. Unless they agree on such ends, the coalition will in time break down through conflicting tactics and goals.

Thirdly, similar status position relative to the economic and political power of the opposition is both desirable and necessary. The parties to the coalition should not be of different economic classes, social castes, social statuses, legal estates, or of any other widely divergent status or power groups. A party that is either economically, socially, or politically of one status is not likely to stay in a coalition with a group of a different status, especially if that status difference has a high value and involves charity from the dominant power groups. Coalitions between such divergent parties break up easily when the security of the party enjoying the most charity becomes threatened. Middle-class whites, for example, have tended to desert blacks whenever their privileged middle-class incomes have become threatened. Whites, in general, have tended to give up their civil-rights advocacy when their racial privileges have come under threat. When white voters have discovered that the enfranchisement of blacks may mean a loss of their racial privileges, they have voted or maneuvered to disfranchise blacks. It should be clear that blacks have been held back by many of the same whites who claim they want equality for all. Different status positions have caused splits in goals and ultimate ends of blacks and whites. It is very clear that the parties to a coalition ought to stand in the same or in an equivalent status relationship to the opposition, or their mutual commitments to racial change will not be maintained to the end.

Fourthly, the parties to a coalition have a greater chance of success if they have the same ideological perspective; that is, if they define the opposition and the conditions under which they live in similar ways. This is not to say that because some whites and blacks define the race situation in the United States similarly, they would make parties to an effective coalition. Many white people in the United States define the social conditions as racially unjust and feel that these injustices are wrong, but they are afraid to act against them. Believing and feeling in similar ways as blacks is not as important as having similar status positions relative to wielders of power. Coalitions are effective if the parties can *act* together for their mutual benefit; they are not necessarily effective simply because the parties hold the same beliefs about their mutual good.

In summary, we may say that attempts at permanent coalitions of black and white sharecroppers, black and white laborers, black and white civil rights workers, black and white college students, and black and white voters have not worked because the prerequisites mentioned above have not been fulfilled. Coalition politics has been of very limited value to blacks in the United States. In all the above instances, whites have pulled out of coalitions because they either did not need the blacks to accomplish their goals or were only vicariously involved in the black struggle and stopped supporting blacks when their own status or power interests became threatened. Whites and blacks have not been locked in interdependent relationships in which the accomplishment of racial goals of whites has been contingent upon blacks also accomplishing their goals. Since whites generally have been powerful and blacks generally have been powerless, whites could choose to stay in or pull out of the racial coalitions at their discretion without serious detriment to the accomplishment of their political goals and economic interests. Black-white coalitions can work only under very particular conditions.

The single most important coalition in the American black experience has been that which occurred between the blacks of African appearance and the blacks of European appearance. The European-looking blacks and the African-looking blacks have come to define their goals, ultimate ends, beliefs, and sentiments as the same. Why? One answer is that these two racially distinct groupings (one essentially Negroid and the other essentially Caucasian) were forced into exactly the same social, economic, and political relationship vis-a-vis the white supremacists. The white supremacists structured the United States' economic, political, and social institutions in a way that Caucasian types of African ancestry had the same estate and caste status as the Negroid types. The racial laws effectively defined the European-looking persons as blacks and subjected them to the same legal and social restrictions as the African-looking persons, also defined as blacks. Even those persons of only one-fourth, one-eighth, or one-sixteenth African descent found that they could not relieve their estate and caste condition of slavery, political disfranchisement, or lack of freedom from racial discrimination without relieving these conditions for those of full African descent. White supremacists forced these near-whites and pure blacks together into a contingency relationship that gave rise to similar goals, ends, beliefs, and sentiments. The hybrids were made to stand in exactly the same legal status position as were pure blacks relative to those classified as whites. This relationship and this socially structured contingency caused two racially distinguishable groupings to unite in a coalition with common goals, common strategic interests, and common beliefs and sentiments. This coalition has lasted for more than one hundred years, and is growing more consanguine day by day.

Carmichael and Hamilton on the other hand have claimed that viable coalitions stem from four preconditions:

1. The recognition by the parties involved of their respective self-interests.

2. The mutual belief that each party stands to benefit in terms of that self-interest from allying with the other or others.

3. The acceptance of the fact that each party has its own independent base of power and does not depend for ultimate decision making on a force outside itself.

4. The realization that the coalition deals with specific and identifiable goals as opposed to general and vague goals.

This author would go beyond mutual recognition, belief, acceptance, and realization. Mutualities are important, but more important are interdependence, contingency, and common status position of class, power, and privilege. It seems that the only truly viable racial coalitions have occurred when these latter preconditions have been fulfilled among the parties to the coalitions.[1]

Assimilation

In the past, blacks have tried to overcome their inferior statuses by copying the manners, morals, thought processes, and emotional responses of the dominant group. Having believed that social and psychological transformations were required, many acquiesced in order to change their racial conditions in the U.S. White gatekeepers have so often told blacks that their inferior moral and social position is a result of their physical and psychological traits, that many have assumed that their inequalities in economic success, educational achievement, and power attainment were causes of racial discrimination, rather than the effects of discrimination in estate, caste and class.

Many assimilationist blacks have accepted the dominant group's values of success, morals, beauty, and other qualities, and by comparison have deduced that they were indeed inferior, and that individual betterment was the way to improve their racial status. Accordingly, for a time they have accepted the myth that their racial status was self-induced even in the face of the fact that they enjoy only privileges assigned by law and custom and violently enforced by white law enforcement personnel. However as these most educated, most white-wardly mobile, and most affluent blacks have been blatantly and forcibly excluded from various dominant-group activities, neighbor-hoods, and organizations because of their racial origins, they have been brought to the conclusion in striving to change their condition that they occupy an estate status which is involuntary, not voluntary, which is assigned, not achieved, and which cannot be changed by the individual alone but only law. They have finally learned that the monopoly of white force and power has been most instrumental in maintaining racial discrimination. They have finally learned that their personal, innate deficiencies have had nothing to do with their status deprivations.

Dominant-subordinate relationships of great pervasiveness and longevity have usually been based on one or more visible character-istics, like race. Racially visible characteristics have historically be-come status designations; that is, they have become like brands which identify the origins of individuals, regardless of their achievements in education, occupation, manners, or morals. Since racial appearance has usually been so unchangeable, social statuses based on these biological marks have become just as immutable. Even when technological advancement has permitted biological characteristics like skin color, hair texture, hair color, nose shape, eye color, and height to be changed, force and violence has been used to maintain the racial estates and caste relations. In such cases, the real bases of racial statuses have been legal and social ascription not achievement.

Those blacks who have copied whites have been only symbolically equal in behavior, in material acquisition, and in appearance. Legally they have been subordinate to the dominant-group members and thus have had to painfully learn that the symbols of status do not substitute for the substance of status. Racial status in the U.S. has been based on skin color and racial origins, with the result that the acquisition of material symbols of status does not change the assigned racial status of blacks or any other racial minorities. Many more blacks need not, therefore, go through this experience only to encounter double and triple failure—to discover that the symbolic clothing of status does not make a man of that status in substance—in law.

Individual improvement or economic betterment activities, however, can be positively useful in an open society, that is, a society based on acquirable characteristics or skills. But when racial status positions are based on inherited characteristics such as biological origin, then individual striving becomes a matter of misplaced emphasis. Individual striving does not alter the status-by-origin condition. All those of the same origin must overcome it together because class status and estate and caste status are different realities. Individuals can achieve high class status and still occupy a low estate and caste status. Honor, privilege, and respect for blacks in the United States follow primarily from racial origins not material achievements. When dominant-group members say, "No matter how high you rise, you are still a nigger, a kike, a Polack," they are referring to status-by-origin. When they say, "If you're white, you're all right; if you're brown, you can hang around; but if you're black, get back!" White people are talking about status-by-origin. Blacks, by reason of origin, are categorically treated alike, regardless of class achievement.

Using a status-by-origin system, the dominant group can cause even the most capable members of the subordinate group to fail. The dominant group can raise or change qualification criteria, so that personal deficiency will seem to have caused the failure. The dominants can cause failure whenever they wish to deny full and equal participation to blacks. They can always "prove" that racial deficiencies caused the failure. Minorities thereby become confused as to the real causes of their conditions. But a few minority-group members, by engaging in the individual-betterment process, test the system to show that large numbers of them need not go through the same failures in order to learn that no particular type of personality, no particular level of intelligence, or no particular form of acculturation or achievement is sufficient to change the collective racial status. Collective, total, and categorical discrimination perpetrated by the dominant group produces the discrepancy between the black man's innate capacities and his actual achievements. The solution therefore is one of partial or total reconstruction of society, not individual improvement.

System reconstruction is the answer. Blacks must reconstruct all parts of the estate and caste system which allocates honor, power, and privilege on the basis of status-by-origin, for such criteria predetermine group successes and failures. Such criteria predetermine what categories of people will generally succeed, and what categories will partially succeed, and what categories will completely fail. Estates in American have predetermined that blacks fail. Blacks must therefore eliminate those ascriptive processes which cause failure; otherwise, individual improvement activities can be no more than empty motions—a treadmill race.

Integrationism

The doctrine presently under attack is one of the so-called periods of "integrationism." "Integration" can refer to different social realities. For example, an integrated society can mean an open society in which people have choices restricted only by their personal preferences, prejudices, and skills. An open society permits and defends equal opportunities, liberties, and rights for all. Black or white, citizens in such a society act without fear of reprisals by law or by mob rule. An open society is truly an achievement-oriented society where all persons, regardless of race, are given equal chances, relative to objective opportunities, to realize their abilities without being artificially restricted by biological (racial) origins. In such a society, most people believe that where there's a will, there's a way, since everyone has an equal opportunity to succeed—that hard work, individual improvement, self-sacrifice, and ambition are all it takes to succeed.

But integration did not come to mean openness; it came to mean token desegregation, quota mixing, and racial balance, a minimal change in estate and caste conditions. It came to mean whatever whites, and whites alone, desired and were willing to accept at the time. By their control over school boards, local government, and local law enforcement, whites determined the meaning of integration and enforced it. What they did not like, they did not implement. Overall, they defined the meaning, terms, and rate of integration, as well as the sacrificial populations who would be "integrated" for appearances of conforming to law and creed.

Up to now, integration has been white-controlled, white-dominated, and white-led. It has become still another form of white supremacy. Racism has been the basic principle running through all decisions. Individual opportunities for blacks have not been equitable or equalized by integration, and many freedoms have been taken away rather than protected.

As in all racially ascriptive systems, status, honor, privilege, and liberty have been defined by the dominant group and thus integration also has been defined by the white supremacists. It has been used to limit, place, reward, or punish blacks whenever they wanted to. Since the whites "sponsor" the few blacks who do succeed, and make possible their participation in "the club," whites are ultimately in control of these black "successes." Whatever the number of blacks who participate and whatever their degrees of success they have become dependent on what their white sponsors decide. Any unsolicited attempts by these blacks to increase their number in "the club" beyond what whites allowed, or to achieve more success than what whites permitted, or to exercise more than nominal power meet with either white resistance or nullification, or elimination.

Token integrationism is another covert form of racism. Institutional racism during this epoch has been covertly exercised through budget allocations, bureaucratic regulations, job-qualification standards, promotion criteria, and so on. Racism operates in day-to-day practices and in unwritten policies. For example, while whites have regularly been forced into failing the same qualification tests, integrationists have been using qualification tests not unlike the restrictive literacy tests and understanding tests of the last jim crow epoch. Whites have been the ones determining the test items, scores, and passes and failures. The failure of blacks therefore, has been in large part intentionally contrived via the processes of screening and selection, the first line of contrived failures. Institutions of all types whether they have been public or private, sacred or secular have been using such racist practices. Integration means black subordination to whites.

Under integrationism blacks are not so much entangled in indebtedness and forced to work as they are forced out of gainful employment altogether. Blacks today are not so much kept from going to school as high quality education is kept out of their schools. They are not so much kept from voting as their votes are kept from having their full collective effect. They are not so much denied the right to bring suits to court as they are denied juries and judges of peers which could determine the court outcomes in their favor. In short, integrationist policies have been gradualist, obstructionist, tokenistic, and paternalistic, all of which have been the traditional tactics of racists. Integration has come to mean a *stratified integration*, following the same model of hierarchy as was used in the time of despotism and jim crowism; white over black relations are still the "right" relations between the races even according to the integrationists.

Separatism

For most of their presence in the U.S. blacks have been thwarted in their efforts as individuals to assimilate and integrate. Even though they have been willing to change their behavior and their appearance to coincide with the cultural models of the white group, they have found that the white group has continued either to restrict the degree of their assimilation or to ignore their assimilation. They have found that the dominant group has continued to discriminate on the basis of racial estates rather than on the basis of assimilated or nonassimilation attributes. As a larger and larger number of blacks have found their efforts continually thwarted by devices of tokenism, gradualism, and obstructionism, many have come to conclude that total and full assimilation into a white dominated society is impossible. In such times, they have turned to various types of separatism with hope of realizing their potentialities for self-improvement and collective betterment within black communities or nations.

Communal Separatism

Communal separatism has become for some blacks a means by which to mobilize, organize, and solidify the black population in the United States to the point where they can collectively act for their legal, social, and economic betterment within the territorial and political confines of the U.S. This kind of movement has emphasized the development of "community." Communal separatism has not been an end in itself as much as it has been a means to organize collective activities to overcome the institutional barriers of racial discrimination. This type of movement has joined the ideas of social separation with social and personal betterment. Concretely, black separatists of this type have tried to take control of the basic service institutions of their territory in order to speed up the process of betterment and to increase economic and political opportunities for the advancement of black people. Communal separatism proposes to substitute racial separation for racial integration, and collective striving for individual striving as the mechanisms for racial improvement.

Advocating a communal-betterment approach over an individual-betterment approach as the chief means for racial improvement has had many advantages. For example, communal separatism creates greater opportunities for racial solidarity, value consensus, interpersonal communication, and collective action in the interest of all. On the other hand, the individual-betterment approach has the negative consequences of individualizing the racial struggle, generating individual loyalties, and causing undue emulation of dominant-group models. Another advantage is that communal separatism militates against most of the previous integrationist-assimilationist tendencies and helps generate social closure and racial solidarity rather than racial disintegration.

Blacks have worked out two types of communal separatism. The first type might be called "nonsectarian." This type involves blacks who have turned inward to organize and improve, but according to the institutional models, party politics and capitalism of the dominant group. The real distinctive features of this movement have been its emphasis on community control, separation, and nonrevolutionary goals. Since these type movements have been essentially reformists in respect to ultimate ends, their communities have eventually faded away as distinctive ethnic communities within the larger society, as the younger generations have left and assimilated among the dominant group, and as ventures in social and economic advancement have been successful.

Communal separatism of the nonsectarian type is not an end in itself; it is basically a device by which blacks can act together for their mutual interests. Being discriminated against by estate and caste and being deprived of goods, opportunities, and experiences for advancement, which all humans deserve from time to time, some blacks turn to communal separatism to overcome these racial barriers to *individual mobility*. Permanent national independence, by contrast, is not the ultimate goal. Separatism is valued only as an organizing device to achieve quicker and greater betterment in the opportunity structure of the larger society. Nonsectarian separatists mostly want to participate more fully in the mainstream of society and rarely do they reject white offers for full participation. Legal and customary exclusion force upon them a realization of collective barriers to advancement, and this realization forces on them a collective consciousness, which in turn gives rise to collective sentiments of resentment. These sentiments bring forth collective protest actions, which in turn produce collective assaults on the racially discriminatory institutions. Once opportunities for advancement become sufficiently available, one by one the minority-group members leave the ethnically separated community in order to seek their individual fortunes in the larger society. As they integrate and acculturate, their identification with the ethnic community wanes. Among them, collective actions become less and less important, and individual efforts for social improvement become primary. Group unity wanes; in-group value consensus breaks down, and in-group discipline becomes ineffective. Eventually, the black population completely disperses residentially and socially throughout the institutions of the larger society.

The second type of communal separatism can be called "sectarian."

This type of separatism has become not only a means to betterment but also a desired end in itself. Sectarian movements have been concerned about uniting the individuated black population which occupies a designated territory. However, the ultimate objective of this unity has not been to corral the power to create opportunities for wider assimilation in the white dominated society, but to develop unity and power for more independence from white domination. Sectarian movements have started developing distinctive cultural features and distinctive service institutions which the people themselves own, control, and operate. Sectarian blacks, for example, have tried to work out new and distinctive institutional ways for child socialization, motivation management, decision making, goal achievement, social control, recruitment, and boundary maintenance. As sectarians, they have tried, in essence, to raise in relief bio-cultural differences between themselves and white people outside the community by cultivating among blacks distinctive dieties, language, and behavioral rituals, ideologies, and values.

What is true for the nonsectarian movement is true for communal separatism of the sectarian variety, which is also oriented to group improvement; community separatism and community control over the basic institutions are critical means for sectarians to improve the group as a whole. The same in-group advantages which accrue to the nonsectarian communalists accrue to the sectarian separatists as well: for example, heightened group loyalties, group interests, and group identification. Increased racial self-sufficiency, self-legitimation, and self-determination are, however, even better achieved through sectarianism.

Contrary to popular rhetoric, most of these communal-separatism movements have not had revolutionary ends. They have not been oriented toward a total reconstruction of the larger society, but instead they have been either societal reform movements or withdrawal movements. Sectarian separatists have eschewed close involvement in reconstructionist, reformist, or revolutionary movements. Sectarians have usually withdrawn and insulated themselves from the larger concerns of the nation or the world. In doing so, they have survived independently so long as they could remain relatively self-sufficient socially and economically, and so long as they could avoid overt conflicts with the dominant group. When conflict has been unavoidable, these groups have voluntarily left the society or they have been forcefully banished from the society by the dominant group. Being sectarians within a hostile society, such groups have been just as

unprotected as assimilationist blacks as far as enjoying the same inalienable rights guaranteed to white men and women. The dominant
group has been capable of and inclined toward denying the enjoyment of those inalienable rights in any black group. Thus, even the
communal separatists of the sectarian variety, like other blacks, have
been forced to operate to some extent within the institutional racism
of the larger society. They have, however, striven very hard to conform
only minimally and to increase their economic sufficiency so as to
maximize their social and cultural independence, if not their political independence, from the larger society. While such radical withdrawals have increased the groups' chances for social autonomy, this
autonomy has been a matter of degree. It must be emphasized that
communal separatism of blacks within a white society still has left
black groups territorially, politically, and economically under the
control of the dominant group.

On balance, communal separatism of any type gives individual
blacks more degrees of freedom than would the establishment of closer
social and political alliances with white groups. Interracial alliances,
with all the dependencies they entail, lessen black autonomy; that
is, they lessen blacks' capacities to act completely on their own without
compromising with other groups. Communal separatism maximizes
the chances that black people *within* the United States can exclusively
control the basic service institutions of their communities, such as
commercial establishments, schools, courts, churches, and government.
Sectarian separatists do not seek to overturn, reform, or control the
existing institutions. They seek rather to withdraw from the societal
institutions and develop their own communal institutions in order
to foster a collective autonomy and to improve the collective socioeconomic and political conditions of their racial group. As such, they
have the only good chance for blacks to realize the relative autonomy
sought by true separatists.

It should be pointed out for purposes of emphasis that communal
separatist movements do involve integration at some levels, but the
integration is collective rather than individual; communities are the
units of integration rather than individuals. Communal integration
permits interethnic cooperation and coexistence without the usual
costs of erasing racial identities or melting down the varieties of
cultures into one cultural amalgam. Those arguing about whether or
not more blacks should become separatist rather than integrationist
need to examine their ultimate values. Blacks and whites must decide
explicitly whether they want a society with or without distinct races

and cultures. Integration with bio-cultural differences is possible through communal separatism providing that the regional or metropolitan governments operate with equity at all times.

National Separatism

National separatists, in contrast to communal separatists, are collectives of people who seek territorial and political independence from the jurisdiction of the U.S. With both territorial and political independence, nationhood becomes a possibility. Territorial sovereignty and political independence are two of the prerequisites of nationhood. Without these, there is only pseudo-nationhood.

National separatists divide along the same lines as communal separatists, namely, along nonsectarian and sectarian lines. Nonsectarians seek to transplant the culture and institutions of the dominant group in another territorially and politically independent area. They seek to withdraw from the U.S. because they have found their economic life-chances or political rights despotically restricted by the institutional leaders and officials of the larger society. Through national independence, the nonsectarians hope to fulfill their dreams of unlimited economic and political betterment—something they cannot do under the jurisdiction of the dominant group.

Such nationalistic movements are in most instances nonrevolutionary because they simply seek to emigrate from rather than to control the existing institutions of the larger society. Most usually they do not attempt to institute a new and distinctive set of institutions or a new culture; they seek only to improve the plight of the whole people through the same type of institutions and culture as the dominant group has, but they plan to do it on a different land mass where they are sovereign.

Sectarian nationalists, by contrast, seek a territorial and political withdrawal in order to do two things: first, to be territorially and politically independent of the dominant society of which they are a part; and secondly, to realize a distinctive culture and to operate a distinctive set of institutions so as to set themselves free economically, culturally, socially, and psychologically. Sectarian national separatists are just like sectarian communal separatists except that the former seek complete territorial and political independence in addition to a separate cultural identity as a people.

The nationalists in general are more independence-minded than the communalists. They seek complete liberation from the U.S.

society, not token freedom. They seek the true *separate* development. Communalists use the rhetoric of separate development, but they seek *concordant* development within the parent society, according to which, the dominant group would remain in control of them. It would control the black aggregate demand for labor and products, their supply of capital and raw materials, and their economic policies, foreign and domestic. The nationalists have a better plan for maximizing liberation and autonomy. Nations are not completely without dependencies, nor are they completely dependent either. Communities are in all ways and at all times dependent. Communal separatism still amounts to white containment and domination. Communalism of all types involves integration at some level and hence all of the insidiousness of integrationism American style.

Revolutionary Nationalism

Revolutionary nationalism is quite different from either communal or national separatism. Revolutionary nationalists seek to turn out of office the present racist leaders and to change the institutions of the larger society in the interests of all. These blacks would like to acquire the instruments of coercion and influence to take control of the institutions and transform them according to new models of non-capitalistic democratic socialism.

What is distinctive about such nationalists is the fact that revolutionary nationalists neither seek to withdraw to a separate territory nor to control and run the same old "decadent" institutions. Instead, they seek to acquire a monopoly of political and physical force to achieve sovereignty over the existing territory and institutions, and, once control is established, they plan to transform the "decadent" racist institutions of the existing society into a new more equitable nonracial order. Unlike palace revolutionaries who seek only to overthrow the existing leaders of institutions and run these existing "decadent" institutions in their own interests without an eye to transforming the institutional order and culture of the existent society, revolutionary nationalists seek the leadership to transform the decadent institutions. They seek liberation from oppressive men and women, and liberation from oppressive institutions and insist on subplanting them with some things and some people who are more democratic and equitable.

The basic shortcoming of revolutionary nationalists is that they either usually do not have widespread popular support, or, even if they have widespread popular support, they do not have sufficient control over the means of force and violence to prevent a reactionary movement. Revolutionary blacks in the U.S. are a good case in point: they are too separated from control over the means of force and violence, in addition to not enjoying popular white support for their ends. Even though many whites are economically deprived, their prejudices cause them to defend the status quo with their lives, thus leaving black revolutionaries with only sufficient power to challenge the present power structure, but not sufficient power to seize and control the whole institutional system.

Revolutionary nationalists come in two varieties: One variety are black nationalists, meaning that they want a black dominated nation. They are sometimes sectarian and sometimes nonsectarian in orientation. Whatever they may be, they cannot expect biracial support for their revolution in the U.S. On the other hand, another variety of revolutionary nationalists are non-racially oriented. They expect and want all "oppressed" categories white and black to coalesce, rise up and take control of the present means of production and governance. They believe that economic exploitation is at the base of racial deprivation. They see that racism as a kind of classism, and that capitalism produces racial and economic classism and some will even maintain that capitalism produces sexism as well. If the root of all types of classism is capitalism, it follows that all these non-capitalists must overthrow the capitalists in order to eradicate all the inequities and exploitation in the U.S. The logical conclusion is that the revolutionary nationalists must be integrationists and must come from various racial, sexual and economic groups. The error of this analysis is that estate and caste divisions which produce differential life-chances for betterment make it impossible for there to be a sustained broad alliance between unequal groups such as whites and blacks, men and women. The necessary interlocking contingent relationships do not exist and hence cooptation and conflict within ranks is easily produced by the dominant group. A union of separate ethnic republics is the best alternative goal for the various racial minorities living presently in the confines of the U.S. Simultaneous ethnic nationalist assaults seems probable and profitable to pursue.

SUMMARY

Blacks have moved through three historic periods, each of which has been dominated by specific and outstanding political and economic

doctrines. Historically, blacks have not been singular in their political and economic thinking; that is to say, they have espoused several
political-economic doctrines—at times, several within a single period.
Nevertheless, each period has generally been dominated by one particular political economic doctrine. For example, the first period, from
1660 to the Emancipation Proclamation, was dominated by the doctrine of black abolitionism. The second period, from the end of the
Civil War to 1877, was a time of black assimilationism. The third
period, from 1878 to the Meredith freedom march in Mississippi, was
dominated by neo-abolitionism and neo-assimilationism. Finally, the
fourth period, from the Meredith freedom march to the present, has
been dominated by black separatism.

Within each of those historical periods, there were persons espousing assimilation, separation and revolution but never with equal
force; that is, each period was always dominated by one or the other
economic and political doctrine.

In view of the white adversary, this was as it should be, since social
movements must adapt to the social-structural realities confronting
them. There is always an action-reaction relationship between a movement and institutions. In practice, institutions select and form, make
powerful or impotent a select few leaders of the masses within each
historical period. Thus minority group individuals who are moved
to act can produce modifications using the regular institutional
forces. And so it has been with blacks in America; through one or
another set of institutional forces, they have changed still other institutions with various strategies, and activities. Blacks have moved toward, against, or away from institutions depending on the institutional
pressures operating at the time. Blacks have not always been totally
successful, but they have always been totally active in one manner or
another for three hundred and more years in their own liberation.

To be sure, blacks could not have succeeded by acting according to
only one strategy. There have been ideological differences among
blacks from the beginning because differences in social conditions
have caused different blacks to approach the matter of liberation in
different ways, such as for example, freed blacks and enslaved blacks
who usually had different options.

Slaves were defined in the laws as things; thus they were not regarded
as persons and had no rights as human beings. They had no legal
way of acting in institutionalized political ways since they had no
institutionalized human presence. They were legally things owned,
controlled, and directed by masters. They had no rights of appeal, or

due process since they had no legal personhood which had to be respected. Being deprived in this manner, violent and nonviolent rebellions were usually the only modes of political-economic liberation available to them.

Freed blacks, on the other hand, in most of the same states could petition the courts through white sponsors for redress of grievances or for the abolition of legal slavery over loved ones. The usual practice in slave-holding states was to deny freed blacks these civil rights exercised by freed white citizens. Freed blacks, in other words, were not as "free" as whites. For this reason, freed blacks also had legitimate reasons for coalescing with slaves. They soon learned that they were being kept as near-slaves and that their own liberation was contingent upon the liberation of all blacks. This contingent relationship was so complete that neither enslaved nor freed could change their positions without changing the conditions for all. This is a reason freed blacks were among the most active abolitionists, in fact, many were the leaders in the abolition movement. They had common vested interests with the enslaved blacks, common socioeconomic and sociopolitical goals. But, more importantly, they had an interlocking dependency which could not be separated without bettering the conditions of all blacks. This was a classic example of the socially imposed coalition.

As we have said, blacks have not been singular in their approach to liberation because they have not had singular conditions facing them. Freed blacks at various times had ways to petition courts and legislatures. They had the right to hire themselves out, keep their earnings, and spend the money any way they wanted. They had much more freedom of movement from one geographical area to another. They had more access to printing equipment and materials and to institutions of learning.

Were it not for such variations in the black liberation struggle, blacks would not have succeeded so well. And were it not for the disunity of whites and hence the misapplications of rules, blacks would not have found social, psychological, legal, and geographical spaces for attacking the system. Dissension among whites left openings where blacks were able to step in and widen the breach. For example, when blacks could not fight from outside, they used white intermediaries; when they could not do this, they made strategic withdrawals to the woods, the swamps, the cities, or to other countries. From each of these vantage points, blacks persisted in assaulting the white system. The weapons the blacks fashioned were out of whatever material was available: sometimes a speech, sometimes a pamphlet, sometimes a knife, sometimes a torch, sometimes a petition, and sometimes their own flesh and blood. Blacks were constantly in revolt in some form or fashion, by active and passive resistance.

The question has been raised as to what the future responses of the black estate are likely to be. The answer is certainly going to be determined by what the future historical conditions will be. If, for example, the historical conditions give rise to a biracial revolutionary movement in which white radicals begin to try to overthrow the present capitalist-imperialist-racist power elite, then it is very possible that the black response will be violent and revolutionary. Revolutionary nationalism is not dead, even though it is being held in abeyance at the present time. With the proper historical conditions, many of the blacks who have been espousing assimilation-integration or separation-emigration would opt for violent revolution. Secondly, if the historial conditions became such that the society becomes more open, allowing blacks more economic, political, social, and educational participation in the larger social system, then it is very possible that the separation-emigration ideology of many will be abandoned for some type of assimilation-integration ideology. It does not seem that the black masses would like to be revolutionary, since it would probably evoke the white response of elimination, mutilation or legal-political repression by the white power structure. The most likely outcome of the racial dialectic in this country will be some type of voluntary separatism wherein blacks and whites can voluntarily segregate in selected spheres of life. That is to say, in areas of private clubs, churches, entertainment, residency, and the like, blacks and whites will have the legal options to voluntarily separate, but in areas where people have to shop, work, and learn and in governmental and judicial spheres where people have to vote, serve in public positions as judges and jurors, blacks and whites will have to integrate. The most formal separation is national separation. If voluntary separatism, which is really communal separatism, fails, national separation will be the ultimate direction of the black liberation movement in the U.S. Abolitionism, assimilationism and communal separatism may not bring complete liberation, but national separatism will and that lesson is yet to be learned.

CONCLUSION

Black liberation strategies have been direct reactions to racist legal-political estates. In the earliest decades of the colonies, white racists used political despotism and chattel slavery to first subjugate and then exploit blacks. They subjugated by divesting blacks of equal rights and exploited by forcibly extracting their labors from them. Blacks challenged these practices and came to use violent and nonviolent sabotage, strikes, work slowdowns, and even assassination when they could. They also used the more institutional means like litigation and legislation when they were available. With a constant unbroken string of attacks on the slavocracy, blacks helped to force the confrontation between the North and the South which resulted in the Civil War.

Contributing to the confrontation which resulted in war and after joining the war to end chattel slavery, they helped abate for a time white despotism as it had been practiced in the South. During the so-called period of reconstruction, blacks embarked on widespread programs of self-help and self-improvement in social, political, economic, and legal ways. White Reconstructionism came to be accelerated by black assimilationism. Quickly blacks moved into the polities, economies, academies, sodalities and churches of the South. But because this improvement was at the expense of white privileges and white birthrights, whites rebelled with terrorism and mob violence. Chiefly by these lawless devices, they coerced, intimidated and murdered enterprising young blacks who sought the fruits of their labors and of their birthright as citizens of the U.S. Whites reverted back to the days of urban slavery and reconstructed the system of jim crow segregation and debt and wage peonage. These were to be the manifestations of political despotism and economic exploitation for the next fifty to seventy-five years depending on what part of the U.S. one is describing. Blacks again came under a despotic racist system of racial estates, castes and classes. Though outnumbered and facing a ruthless enemy with a monopoly of force and violence, blacks were not to be perpetually denied their rights. They mounted a new assault using the double pronged attack of neo-abolitionism and neo-assimilationism. They called out the legalists, the shock troopers, the social workers, and the politicians. They used litigation, legislation, emigration, violent and nonviolent direct action, and other means to raze the walls of segragation and exploitation. Jim crowism and debt peonage have just about been relinquished as devices for holding blacks back and down.

Whites started to retreat to new fortifications. They themselves changed from agricultural to industrial people and hence changed their places of residency too. They called upon a system worked out during the days of industrial slavery—token integrationism and wage peonage. Integrationism was the political mechanism of recruitment and cooptation, and wage peonage was the economic means of exploitation. Blacks were brought into manual labor and paid lower wages than whites doing the same or inferior jobs with inferior skills and training. Though blacks were restricted to the lower paying jobs and the least esteemed jobs, they, however, refused to be denied their just due.

Blacks attacked the practices of token integration with black separatism. Blacks decided that they would have to start their own projects of self-improvement and betterment. They were already in the ghettos and they were already separated from ownership and control of the means of production, distribution and political administration. They did not want to be controlled from outside their reservations: they rebelled, burning, looting, disrupting and generally forcing whites to compromise. Whites conceded the ghetto reservations which were decaying and disorderly. They even helped some black organizations start betterment projects to contain the blacks in the ghettos. With the help of whites blacks trapped themselves because while they pushed separatism, whites pushed containmentism. Now whites would cut off busing black children out of the ghetto and would oppose open-housing legislation. Projects for minority businesses and model cities would be two new programmatic forms of containmentism. Coupled with the wage peonage, whites would still maintain their white-over-black control. This time, it would be less by estates than by caste and class mechanisma. This is the epoch in which blacks find themselves today.

It is puzzling why blacks have not considered that there is hardly a collectivity of 25 million people in the world of any color more educated, more industrialized, more urbanized, more politicized, than the Afro-Americans. If they were to start their own nation, it would begin as one of the most developed nations of the world. Afro-Americans however seem to want to integrate. The question is will they be so militant that they can make the leaders of the U.S. institute a truly open society with no legal or bureaucratic rules subjugating people because of their religion, sex, race, or occupation? Short of revolutionary openism, the political deprivation and economic exploitation of blacks in America will continue indefinitely. Anything short of reconstruction programs will result in the perpetuation of the white-over-black institutions in one form or another. Such a reconstruction I believe is in the future of these United States of America.

Bibliographic Essay

The ultimate purpose of my book is to examine the liberation activities of the Afro-American over the past 300 and more years. To do this, I did not necessarily go to primary sources such as slave narrators, personal letters of slave holders, or government documents. I was quite satisfied to use secondary sources, chiefly monographs, to try to discern what the patterns of the liberation struggle were. As they turned out, the struggles were very varied in form; the measures used by white supremacists were numerous and varied, and so the counter measures used by blacks, of necessity, were also numerous and varied. It turned out that there were no nationwide campaigns coordinated and directed by central black directorate. The struggles, I discovered, turned out to be a multiplicity of individual efforts uncoordinated, untimed, undirected, and quite situational. The books which were used together revealed this pattern of liberation activities. I uncovered a natural history of the liberation activities which validated my implicit hypothesis, namely, that free men set themselves free.

There have been many myths written about how the Afro-American accepted his slave condition and hence was contented and happy in a condition of permanent servitude; these myths made it impossible to understand the black revolts of the 1960's. My study has been an attempt to show that the black revolts of the 1960's were not isolated events, but were, in fact, part of 300 years of liberation activities which began even before the moment of judicial and customary slavery and continued throughout the total period of statutory slavery and beyond. Blacks have revolted in numerous ways, sometimes in imperceptible ways, if one is looking for overt, violent direct-action as a typical response to oppression in the United States.

The History of Slavery in Virginia by James C. Ballagh is a most useful book because more than any other source it details the step by step evolution from customary slavery through judicial to statutory slavery in British America. In addition, this book is one of the few sources that discusses white slavery as well as Indian slavery, showing the precedents for African slavery which eventually became the dominant labor system in both the North and the South in the early days of British America. Significantly Ballagh's book shows and documents the fact that statutory recognition of slavery originated in the North and not in the South, and that Virginia, the most famous of the slave states, was really the third state to give legal recognition to slavery. Closely related to this book is *The Free Negro in Virginia* by John H. Russell. One of the main contributions of the book is that it traces law by law the regression from an egalitarian-looking society to a totalitarian racist society. His book, by focusing on the freed blacks, revealed what the future position of blacks was to be in this New World society as early as 1675. Russell's book shows clearly that white nationalism, Anglo-Saxon conformity, white supremacy, white racism, and white privileges were to be the cornerstones of British America. A second important history of constitutional racism in Mary Frances Berry's *Black Resistance/White Law* in which Supreme Court decisions and presidential executive orders are reviewed, analyzed and evaluated. All have been found guilty of racism in this book. In addition, *American Slave Code*, by William Goddell presents a compilation of the various laws defining and regulating slavery, including the relations between slaves and slave masters. This book perhaps more than any other documents the statutory nature of the U.S. system of racial stratification which to my mind adds up to a system of racial estates. I also found Ulrich B. Phillips' book, *American Negro Slavery*, to be well documented. If we recognize that the author was an avowed racist and took pro-southern pro-slavery view of slavery, then it is easier to understand his conclusions and distinguish them from fact. Separating his ideology from the facts, the reader will find this an informative book.

Eugene D. Genovese's book *The Political Economy of Slavery* is an excellent discussion of the economic aspects of slavery and how the rebellious behavior of slaves decreased the profitability of the slave labor system. The book examines the pros and cons of the profitability of slavery, explores various hypotheses, and draws very definitive conclusions. Genovese's book was most useful to me, however, in identifying the many ways slaves sabotaged the system. *North of Slavery* by Leon F. Litwack reports on how blacks were treated in the North before and after the abolition of slavery in the North. This book presents supporting evidence to Phillips' study about the free blacks in Virginia and confirms that the avowed intentions of the early settlers of this country were to make this society and to keep this society Anglo-dominated. In *North of Slavery*, Litwack points up just how weak egalitarianism was in the North, and how strong racism operated in all parts of the North with and without the demands of slavery. Robert S. Starobin's *Industrial Slavery in the the Old South* is especially important because it documents how industrial corporations participated in maintaining slavery rather than eradicating it. Even though industrial slavery was very limited, it was important to the early industrial enterprises in the South and helped to give rise to such sociological ventures as stratified integration and wage peonage. In fact, industrial slavery is the first stage of development wherein wage peonage becomes an institutionalized practice of the American industrialists.

Slavery in Cities , by Richard Wade is an excellent study of the opportunities, the life chances and the life styles of both freed and enslaved blacks who were in the ante-bellum southern cities. Wade thoughtfully compares slaves in the city with slaves in the country and shows how the methods of control on work and on movement differed between urban and rural slave systems. With this comparative focus, the book is especially informative about the roots of the jim crow system of segregation which was to be fully institutionalized thoughout the South around the turn of the century.

There are several books which influenced my thinking that do not necessarily appear in the footnotes: one is *David Walker's Appeal*, edited by Charles M. Wiltse, which is a rabid attack on slavery by this freed black. David Walker shows how a large segment of blacks felt about slavery and what measures they entertained to force a redress of their grievances and for getting the complete freedom. A second book which influenced me was James T. Holly and J. Dennis Harris' *Separatism in the Caribbean*, 1860. This documentary account tells of attempts by a select group of Afro-Americans to emigrate to Haiti in the late 1850's and early 1860's. The book is important because it sets out in clear and concise terms what the grievances were that blacks had at that time and how they deliberated over the various alternatives for alleviating their oppression. This book ought to lay to rest the idea that blacks did not want to leave America, that they preferred the degradation of slavery to the life chances of freedom elsewhere in the world.

Another book which helped me immensely is Lerone Bennett, Jr.'s

Pioneers in Protest. This book presents short biographies of black freedom fighters, both male and female. It shows that freedom does not just happen, but that human beings make history when they take charge of their own liberation to free themselves from the shackles that bind them. These short biographical essays point out the interpenetration of biography and the changing history of society. Benjamin Quarles' *Black Aboltionists* is another very good account of the historical figures and their abolition activities and efforts; it is perhaps the best penetration on the subject in the literature today. This book surveys black litigation, legislation, guerrilla warfare, and how these activities changed the racist system in the face of white resistance at all levels from the grass—roots to capitol hill. The best studies of slave revolts are Herbert Aptheker's *American Negro Slave Revolts, To be Free: Studies in American Negro History,* and *Nat Turner's Slave Rebellion.*

A very important book is Gunner Myrdal's *The American Dilemma,* which is a socio-historical analysis of slavery and the post-slavery eras in the United States. It is especially useful in documenting the measures that whites have used to obstruct, opppress and obliterate blacks to maintain white ·supremacy, while at the same time espousing an egalitarian value system. Myrdal's work is one of the most important and detailed studies of the white-over-black system in the literature.

A book which influenced me greatly was Lerone Bennett Jr.'s *Confrontation in Black and White* which documents the early Jamestown experiences of blacks. Lerone Bennett Jr. concludes that once blacks and whites lived in a substantially open society which later became closed according to racial principles. This book also reviews the black struggles before and since the Civil War and points up the path to liberation blacks have taken.

One very important book spelling out the history of black Americans primarily through biographies is Richard Bardolph's book, *The Negro Vanguard.* The book covers the period from 1700 through 1959 and does a very thorough job of presenting the variety of black experiences through the lives and the struggles of hundreds of black freedom fighters. It is the most detailed history of this kind that I have come across.

The second major period of black struggle was during the so-called reconstruction period. After the Emancipation Proclamation and after the Civil War, blacks found new opportunities to advance themselves in the system, and whites had to find new ways of maintaining their privilege and supremacy. Reconstruction was a time when blacks experimented with more liberation strategies than at any other time in their history in the United States. When one thinks of strategies, one automatically includes rioting and destruction, but rarely do people think of emigration, litigation, legislation, assimilation, education, commercialization as part of a variety of strategies for coping with statutory racism as well as customary racism. The best book that I know of documenting this struggle is W. E. B. DuBois' *Black Reconstruction*. It is one of the most important and well documented studies of black attempts to advance, or let us say rise and advance, in the face of white resistance which included widespread uses of force and violence. Another very important readable book in C. Vann Woodward's *Strange Career of Jim Crow*, which sets out how the jim crow system became institutionalized after the Civil War. The book provides in quick and accessible form the variety of legal and illegal politcal measures whites invented to reverse the gains of black reconstruction.

In Gilbert T. Stephenson's *Racial Distinctions and the Law*, published in 1910, I found perhaps the best available compilation of jim crow laws in the literature. It reviews the racist laws of the North and the South and shows the total range of social discrimination based in law. What is the special contribution of this book is the differentiation between racial distinction by law and racial discrimination by law. Given the fact that the American social system of race relations has been one of statutory racial discrimination, it becomes clear why the black revolts took the character that they took. It is now completely understandable that litigation and legislation movements should be the vanguard movements of all black liberation efforts. It should also be clear that the subjugation of blacks has been led by the polity and politicians who have done more to oppress and exploit blacks than any single segment in American society. *The Betrayal of the Negro* by Rayford W. Logan shows beyond doubt how the polity and politicians acted to make blacks a powerless unprotected group in the society by law and by mob violence and terrorism. The "Betrayal of 1877," as Logan calls it, and the subjugation therefrom for the next fifty years are studied and analyzed in the book, and on the other side of the ledger, the black attempts to resist, protect themselves, and overcome both oppression and degradation are also well presented.

Edwin S. Redkey's *Black Exodus* continues this scenario and tells of the life and struggles of a black nationalist, Henry Turner, who started out as an integrationist and discovered that integration was not really possible in a racist-oriented, pseudo-open society such as the U.S. Along about the turn of the century, he became a black emigrationist predating Garvey by a decade or so and being largely responsible for the basis of emigrationist sentiment that Garvey found when he came to the United States in the 1920's. This book presents evidence of black emigration attempts at the turn of the century and in the early part of this century. A second important book about the struggles of that period is E. Franklin Frazier's *The Black Bourgeoisie*. His book is a scathing attack on the new black middle class that emerged after World War I and World War II. His attack, however, is made by way of comparing the new middle class with the old middle class that came into being after slavery during the early days of black assimiliation and integration. Separating Frazier's ideolgy from the facts he presents, this book becomes a most resourceful socio-historical analysis of the black activities during reconstruction and post-reconstruction period. Because Frazier dealt with urban blacks for the most part, the revolts of black farmers during the reconstruction period and the post-reconsrtuction period were neglected. But in Howard Kester's book, *Revolt Among the Sharecroppers*, I found a very informative analysis of the condition of the sharecroppers, the nature of the sharecropping system, the attempts by rural blacks to enter into coalition with whites to change the system of debt peonages, and also the legal and illegal political measures of capitalists to maintain that exploitative system. This little book stands out as an important study of the southern farmers' unions which emerged at the turn of the last century. More importantly, though, the nature of black debt peonage with all its viciousness is presented and documented in this book.

The third period of black revolts involved a whole series of organizations like the National Afro-American League, the Congress of Racial Equality, the Southern Christian Leadership Conference, the Black Panther Party, the National Welfare Rights Organization, the National Urban League, the National Association for the Advancement of Colored People, the Black Muslims, the Universal Negro Improvement Association and many others. This is a time of abolition activities to eliminate statutory and customary discrimination in the form of jim crow codes; a time for eliminating the artificial and arbitrary denial of black rights and privileges; and a period of attempts by blacks to build up their own institutions as well as force radical change in the existing white controlled, white dominated institutions of the society. One of the most interesting books is Arthur I. Waskow's *Race Riot to Sit-In* based on a study of the NAACP documents. It shows how black strategy evolved from violent riot confrontation to the non-violent confrontation of the early 1960's. A complementary book is Martin Luther King's book, *Stride Toward Freedom* which documents the Montgomery bus boycott and the early days of Civil Rights struggles which led to new developments in the non-violent direct-action strategy made famous by the Southern Christian Leadership Conference.

On the black nationalist side of the ledger, one of the most important forces during this time was Marcus Garvey whose trials and tribulations are documented in Amy J. Garvey, *Garvey and Garveyism*. How and why the Universal Negro Improvement Association failed in its attempt to transport and resettle Afro-Americans back in Africa are amply discussed in this book. Following Garvey and in that same tradition is Elijah Muhammad's *Message to the Black Man*, which presents the origins as well as the ultimate destinies of the black man in America. C. Eric Lincoln's book, *The Black Muslims in America*, is an even better treatment of the ideological as well as the sociological nature of the Black Muslim movement and organization.

Along with the Black Muslims, other organizations have been instrumental in the pursuit of black liberation. Inge Powell Bell, in *CORE: The Strategy of Non-Violence*, presents the early history and philosophy of the Congress of Racial Equality. Since this time, CORE has become a black nationalist, or should I say, black separatist organization which allows violence as a strategy. A second book that presents a quick and brief discussion of a very important liberation group in the black community is *Seize the Time*, by Bobby Seale. He presents the platform, the ends, the objectives, the methods and the chief personalities in the organization when it was at its height of political influence in American society. Bobby Seale, one of the main figures of the Black Panther Party, presents the internal struggles, discipline, and operations within the Black Panther Party which made it a very viable force for a short time in American society. The supreme leader of the Black Panther organization is Huey P. Newton, who has been the chief theoretician of Black Panther ideology. His various writings have been put together in a book entitled, *To Die for the People*. In the book, he spells out the latest position of the Black Panther Party, including criticisms of other contemporary black leaders who are not in agreement with the Party and the most recent attempts to internationalize the struggle along Marxist-Leninist lines. Newton's book is an important statement about the struggles, conflicts and inconsistencies in the Party's rhetoric as well as its behavior.

Howard Zinn has written a book entitled, *SNCC: Student Non-violent Coordinating Committee*. Zinn documents the trials and tribulations that this group went through during the early 60's; it is a narrative about the violence, corruption and degradation of the southern establishment bent on maintaining white supremacy by any means necessary at any cost. It is a well-documented, almost ethnographic, study of the day to day campaigns and struggles of the real live individuals in the rural areas of Alabama and Mississippi who sought to bring change. Another one of the books that was both influential and informative was Hanes Walton Jr.'s *Black Politics*. The book is a socio-political analysis of black participation in the political life of the United States. The book covers both the national as well as regional and local scenes in identifying ideological strategies blacks have been using. Finally, Francis F. Piven and Richard Cloward have written a fine definitive book on recent welfare rights organizations and welfare rights movements entitled *Regulating the Poor*. This book captures more than any other the post-riot activities of black liberation groups and leaders.

Notes

INTRODUCTION: NOTES

1. *Report of the National Advisory Commission on Civil Disorders* (New York: Bantam Books, 1968), p. 1.

2. Gilbert T. Stephenson, *Race Distinctions in American Law* (New York: Johnson Reprint Corp., 1970); James C. Ballagh, *History of Slavery in Virginia* (New York: Johnson Reprint Corp., 1968).

3. Allen D. Grimshaw, ed., *Racial Violence in the United States* (Chicago: Aldine, 1969), p. 28.

4. *Ibid.*, p. 17.

5. Winthrop D. Jordan, *White Over Black* (Baltimore: Penguin Books, 1968), p. 54.

6. See *ibid.*, Chap. III, "Anxious Oppressors," pp. 101-135.

7. William Goodell, *American Slave Code* (New York: Negro Universities Press, 1968), p. 23.

8. *Ibid.*

9. *Ibid.*, p. 290.

10. John H. Russell, *The Free Negro in Virginia: 1619-1865* (Baltimore: John Hopkins University Press, 1913; reprinted New York: Dover, 1969), pp. 88-123.

CHAPTER 1: FOOTNOTES

1. Winthrop D. Jordan, *White Over Black* (Baltimore: Penguin Books, 1968), p. 71.

173

2. *Ibid.*, p. 74.

3. Stanley M. Elkins, *Slavery* 2nd ed. (Chicago: University of Chicago Press, 1968), p. 40.

4. Lerone Bennett, Jr., *Confrontation: Black and White* (Baltimore: Penguin Books, 1966), pp. 96-142; James C. Ballagh, *History of Slavery in Virginia* (New York: Johnson Reprint Corp., 1968), pp. 27-115.

5. Bennett, *op. cit.*, p. 15.

6. *Ibid.*, p. 16.

7. John H. Russell, *The Free Negro in Virginia: 1619-1865* (Baltimore: John Hopkins University Press, 1913; reprinted New York: Dover, 1969); Ulrich B. Phillips, *American Negro Slavery* (New York: Appleton, 1918; reprinted Baton Rouge: Louisiana State University Press, 1966).

8. Ballagh, *op. cit.*, pp. 31-32.

9. *Ibid.*, p. 32.

10. *Ibid.*, p. 34.

11. Jordan, *op. cit.*, p. 75.

12. Albert P. Blaustein and Robert L. Zanpando, *Civil Rights and the American Negro* (New York: Washington Square Press, 1968), p. 9.

13. William Waller Hening, ed., *The Status at Large Being a Collection of All Laws of Virginia from the First Session of the Legislature in the Year 1619* (Richmond, 1809-1823), Vol. 3, No. 13, p. 170.

14. *Ibid.*, p. 460.

15. *Ibid.*, p. 86.

16. *Ibid.*, p. 459.

17. Richard Wade, *Slavery in Cities* (New York: Oxford University Press, 1967), pp. 273-278.

18. *Ibid.*, pp. 90-92.

19. Hening, *op. cit.*, p. 128.

20. *Ibid.*, p. 131.

21. *Ibid.*, pp. 133-134.

22. *Ibid.*, p. 583.

23. *Ibid.*, p. 132.

24. *Ibid.*, p. 127.

25. Jordan, *op. cit.*, p. 79.

26. Hening, *op. cit.*, p. 87.

27. *Ibid.*, p. 454.

28. Gilbert T. Stephenson, *Race Distinctions in American Law* (New York: Johnson Reprint Corp., 1970), p. 19.

29. *Ibid.*, p. 12.

30. *Ibid.*, p. 14.

31. Arnold Rose, *The Negro in America* (New York: Harper & Row, 1964), p. 42.

32. *Ibid.*

33. For the best discussion I have yet found of these phenomena, namely, race-by-appearance and race-by-ancestry, see Oracy Nogueira, "Skin Color and Social Class," in Research Institute for the Study of Man and the Pan American Union, *Plantation Systems of the New World* (Washington, D. C.: Pan American Union, 1959), pp. 164-183.

CHAPTER 2: FOOTNOTES

1. Herbert Aptheker, *American Negro Slave Revolts* (New York: International Publishers, 1968), pp. 56-59.

2. William Hooper Councill, "The Negro Can Grow Only . . . In His Own Sphere, As God Intended," in John H. Bracey, Jr., August Meier, and Elliott Rudwick, *Black Nationalism in America* (Indianapolis: Bobbs-Merrill, 1970), pp. 229-230.

3. *Ibid.*, pp. 228-229.

4. Henry Highland Garnet, "Calls for Slave Rebellions," in John H. Bracey, Jr. *et al.*, *op. cit.*, pp. 70-71.

5. E. Franklin Frazier, *Race and Culture Contacts in the Modern World* (New York: Knopf, 1957), pp. 191-201.

6. Aptheker, *op. cit.*, pp. 60-61.

7. *Ibid.*, p. 67. See also Richard Wade, *Slavery in Cities* (New York: Oxford University Press, 1967), pp. 80-110.

8. Kenneth T. Jackson, *The Ku Klux Klan in the City: 1915-1930* (New York: Oxford University Press, 1970); William Z. Foster, *The Negro People in American History* (New York: International Publishers, 1970), pp. 326-334.

9. Kenneth T. Jackson, *op. cit.*, p. xi.

10. Gunnar Myrdal, *An American Dilemma* (New York: Harper & Row, 1969), pp. 474-504.

11. This section is largely drawn from Leon Friedman, ed., *Southern Justice* (New York: Pantheon, 1955).

12. Robert S. Starobin, *Industrial Slavery in the Old South* (New York: Oxford University Press, 1970), p. 7.

13. Eugene D. Genovese, *The Political Economy of Slavery* (New York: Random House, 1961), p. 21.

14. Ulrich B. Phillips, *American Negro Slavery* (New York: Appleton, 1918; reprinted Baton Rouge: Louisiana State University Press, 1966), p. 305; see also Stanley M. Elkins, *Slavery* 2nd ed. (Chicago: University of Chicago Press, 1968).

15. Phillips, *op. cit.*, p. 360.

16. *Ibid.*

17. *Ibid.*, p. 375.

18. Howard Kester, *Revolt Among the Sharecroppers* (New York: Arno Press and the New York Times, 1969), p. 38.

19. *Ibid.*, pp. 48-49.

20. *Ibid.*, p. 39.

21. *Ibid.*, pp. 39-40.

22. *Ibid.*, pp. 51-52.

23. John Beecher, "The Sharecroppers' Union in Alabama," in *Social Forces*, (Oct. 1934), 13: 124-32.

24. Wade, *op. cit.*, pp. 38-54.

25. Robin Myers, *Black Craftsmen Through History* (New York: Institute of the Joint Apprenticeship Program, 1969), p. 23.

26. *Ibid.*

27. *Ibid.*, p. 22.

28. Starobin, *op. cit.*, pp. 11-12.

29. Peter M. Bergman and Mort N. Bergman, *The Chronological History of the Negro in America* (New York: New American Library, 1969), p. 287.

30. *Ibid.*, p. 304.

31. United States Department of Labor, *The Negroes in the United States: Their Economic and Social Situation* (No. 1511; Washington, D.C.: Government Printing Office, 1966), pp. 28-29.

32. Bureau of the Census and Bureau of Labor Statistics, *The Social and Economic Status of Negroes in the United States, 1970* (No. 394; Washington, D.C.: Government Printing Office, 1971), p. 66.

33. *Ibid.*, p. 63.

34. *Ibid.*, p. 41.

35. John Kenneth Galbraith has done a remarkable job of describing how our system has changed and developed in his *The New Industrial State* (New York: New American Library, 1967).

36. See, for example, Sidney Willhelm, *Who Needs the Negro* (New York: Schenkman, 1970), p. 196.

37. See Bergman and Bergman, *op. cit.*

38. See Rayford W. Logan, *The Betrayal of the Negro* (New York: Macmillan, 1970).

39. Rose Helper, *Racial Policies and Practices of Real Estate Brokers* (Minneapolis: University of Minnesota Press, 1969).

40. See Herbert Hill, "Racial Inequality in Employment: The Patterns of Discrimination," in John F. Kain, *Race and Poverty* (Englewood Cliffs, N.J.: Prentice-Hall, 1969), pp. 78-88.

41. See William K. Tabb, Chap. 3, "Black Power—Green Power," in *The Political Economy of the Black Ghetto* (New York: Norton, 1970), pp. 46-48.

CHAPTER 4: FOOTNOTES

1. Herbert Aptheker, *American Negro Slave Revolts* (New York: International Publishers, 1968), p. 163.

2. Eugene D. Genovese, *The Political Economy of Slavery* (New York: Random House, 1961), p. 112.

3. *Ibid.*, p. 113.

4. Allen D. Grimshaw, ed., *Racial Violence in the United States* (Chicago: Aldine, 1969), p. 101.

5. Arthur I. Waskow, *From Race Riot to Sit-in* (Garden City: Doubleday, 1967).

6. Jerry Cohen and William S. Murphy, *Burn, Baby, Burn* (New York: Dutton, 1966).

7. Philip S. Foner, ed., *The Black Panthers Speak* (New York: Lippincott, 1970).

8. Genovese, *op. cit.*, p. 26.

9. George Washington Williams, *A History of the Negro Race in America* (New York: Bergman Publishers, 1968), p. 164.

10. Mary S. Locke, *Anti-Slavery in America* (New York: Johnson Reprint Corp., 1968), p. 80.

11. *Ibid.*

12. Massachusetts M. S. Archives, Vol. 212, p. 132.

13. Helen T. Catterall, ed., *Judicial Cases Concerning American Slavery And the Negro* (Washington, D.C.: Carnegie Institution, 1936), 4: 413-414.

14. John Daniels, *In Freedom's Birthplace: A Study of Boston Negroes* (New York: Negro Universities Press, 1968), p. 6.

15. Peter M. Bergman and Mort N. Bergman, *The Chronological History of the Negro in America* (New York: New American Library, 1969), p. 259.

16. *Ibid.*, pp. 544-583.

CHAPTER 5: FOOTNOTES

1. Howard H. Bell, "National Negro Conventions of the Middle 1840s; Moral Suasion vs. Political Action," *Journal of Negro History*, 42 (October 1957); 247-260; Leon F. Litwack, "The Emancipation of the Negro Abolitionist," in Martin Duberman, ed., *The Antislavery Vanguard: New Essays on the Abolitionists* (Princeton: Princeton University Press, 1965), pp. 137-155; William H. Pease and Jane H. Pease, "The Negro Convention Movement," in Nathan I. Huggins, Martin Kilson, and Daniel M. Fox, eds., *Key Issues in the Afro-American Experience* (New York: Harcourt Brace Jovanovich, 1971), 1: 191-209.

2. Emma Lou Thornbraugh, "The National Afro-American League, 1887-1908,", *Journal of Southern History*, 28 (November, 1961): 494-512; August Meier and Elliott Rudwick, *From Plantation to Ghetto* (New York: Hill and Wang, 1966), pp. 205-212.

3. Langston Hughes, *Fight for Freedom: The Story of the NAACP* (New York: Norton, 1962); Robert C. Weaver, "The NAACP Today," *Journal of Negro Education*, 29 (Fall, 1960): 421-425.

4. Whitney M. Young, Jr., *To Be Equal* (New York: McGraw-Hill, 1964); L. Hollings Worthwood, "The Urban League Movement," *Journal of Negro History*, 11 (April 1924): 117-126; Kenneth Clark, "The Civil Rights Movement: Momentum and Organization," *Daedalus*, 95 (Winter 1966): 239-267; National Urban League, *The Urban League Story: 1910-1960* (New York: National Urban League, 1961).

5. Edwin S. Redkey, "The Flowering of Black Nationalism: Henry McNeal Turner and Marcus Garvey," in Huggins *et al., op. cit.*, pp. 107-124; E. U. Essien-Udom, *Black Nationalism: A Search for an Identity in America* (Chicago: University of Chicago Press, 1962); E. Franklin Frazier, "The Garvey Movement," *Opportunity*, 4 (November 1926): 346-348.

6. A. Philip Randolph, "A. Philip Randolph Tells . . . 'Why I Would Not Stand for Reelection as President of the National Negro Congress,' " *American Federationist*, 48 (July 1940): 24-25; William Z. Foster, *The Negro People in American History* (New York: International Publishers, 1970), p. 488; Gunnar Myrdal, *An American Dilemma* (New York: Harper & Row, 1969), pp. 817-818.

7. James Farmer, *Freedom—When?* (New York: Random House, 1966); August Meier and Elliott Rudwick, "How CORE Began," *Social Science Quarterly*, 49 (March 1969): 789-799; August Meier, "Negro Protest Movements and Organizations," *Journal of Negro Education*, 32 (Winter 1963): 92-98; Elliott Rudwick and August

Meier, "Organizational Structure and Goal Succession: A Comparative Analysis of the NAACP and CORE, 1964-1968," *Social Science Quarterly*, 51 (June 1970): 9-41.

8. Martin Luther King, Jr., *Stride Toward Freedom: The Montgomery Story* (New York: Harper, 1958); Martin Luther King, Jr., *Why We Can't Wait* (New York: Harper, 1964); Louis E. Lomas, *The Negro Revolt* (New York: Harper, 1962).

9. Charles Jones, "SNCC: Non-violence and Revolution," *New University Thought*, III (September-October 1963), 8-19; Howard Zinn, *SNCC: The New Abolitionists* (Boston: Beacon Press, 1964); Gene Roberts, "The Story of Snick from 'Freedom High' to 'Black Power,' " *New York Times Magazine* (September 25, 1966), pp. 27-29ff.

10. Philip S. Foner, ed., *The Black Panthers Speak* (New York: Lippincott, 1970).

CHAPTER 6 : FOOTNOTES

1. Stokley Carmichael and Charles Hamilton, *Black Power* (New York: Knopf, 1967), pp. 58-85.

INDEX

180